A DISTANT PAST
AN UNCERTAIN FUTURE

A NOVEL

J. R. Klein

D1410259

Publisher: Del Gato
Cover Design: Robin Vuchnich
Editor: Nick May
Library of Congress Control Number: 2019905306
ISBN: 978-1-7339069-2-0
ISBN: 978-1-7339069-3-7 (ebook)

Also by J. R. Klein

Frankie Jones
The Ostermann House

Once again,
for Jeanne

Life is not a matter of holding good cards, but sometimes, playing a poor hand well.

—Jack London

Part I

Chapter One

Every morning at precisely the same time, at exactly the same table, always in the same café, Thomas Blake sits alone drinking coffee. He likes this café because it is where the surfers gather and it makes him feel young to be there. Thomas Blake doesn't feel especially old and he doesn't look especially old. His tanned face and his hair, always slicked back and shiny, make him appear younger than his fifty-six years suggest.

Thomas has dark blue eyes that are full of warmth and friendship. But he knows he is unlike most of the others in the café. They talk about their time on the ocean early in the morning, or the day before, or when they will be there later in the afternoon. Although Thomas will not be there with them, he likes to hear the surfers talk about it.

Thomas Blake is still a strong swimmer and he sometimes feels as though he might be able to get out on the water again, and the thought of that always makes him feel good. He tells himself it's worth a try. He could take his board and paddle out and if nothing else he could float for a while where the swells build into crests that roll to shore and peak into waves good enough to ride. He could do that and breathe the sea mist and then, after a while, paddle to shore without even riding a wave. Doing that would make him feel good. Every day he promises he will, and every day passes without him doing it.

He likes the surfers and he respects their way of life even though most people Thomas's age see them as feckless—wasting the best part of their life on a surfboard out on the blue Pacific. Thomas knows what it's like to be out there, and it annoys him to hear people criticize the surfers that way. He knows what it's like to float with your legs dangling over the board and to hear the weeping wind as it blows across the water. To feel the connection with nature and the ocean. The connection to where, far off in the distance, the water and the sky form a perfect union so that all of Earth—both the surface of it and that which is above it—are seamlessly joined by the ancient federation of creation.

Thomas wants to be out on the water again, but he has lost confidence in that part of his life. And though he was once a man of great confidence, a sense of deep self-doubt has taken hold of him—a feeling that has been growing within him slowly and quietly since his wife died. And so, he loves being around the surfers at the café. The men are handsome and he remembers how in his youth he was like that. The women are beautiful and he remembers how his wife was always beautiful. How her face sparkled with joy the way theirs do now.

The merry eyes of the surfers inspire Thomas to think

young thoughts, and he likes that more than anything. He does not wish to have his youth back again so much as he laments that it is now gone forever. And so Thomas tries to hold onto life in whatever way he can.

Chapter Two

Thomas Blake is a novelist. He has lived in Del Mar, California for twenty-seven years. The large corporation he once worked for as an accountant in Boston transferred him and his wife, Kathryn, to San Diego when they were both twenty-nine. Kathryn passed away three years ago. Thomas still lives in the same small bungalow he and Kathryn bought when they first arrived, when Del Mar was quaint and had a certain angelic simplicity to it.

Soon after coming to Del Mar, Thomas made a vow that he would never spend his whole life punching numbers into a calculator, collecting a paycheck from doing the same thing over and over day after day. His goal was to write great detective novels. He set up a table in his garage and in the mornings before work and for many long hours on weekends he tapped out the words of his first novel.

The garage had large wide doors and two good windows that he could count on to bring in luscious soft breezes. It made him feel good just to be sitting there, and so he rarely thought about any chance of success that might come from his writing efforts.

But then it happened. And like a wave that grows slowly up, rising from far out on the flat ocean as a swell that breaks into a surge, the book became a bestseller. Because of his own introspection, Thomas insisted that it be published under the pen name of Philip Keenly without his picture and without the usual author biography. It made him feel a little like J. D. Salinger, who demanded plain covers devoid of author photos. For decades, the Keenly author became as much a mystery to the world as the stories laid out inside the book.

With the success of his books, the calculator was gone and, despite the large royalty checks that periodically rolled in, Thomas and his wife continued living in their simple bungalow in Del Mar on Tenth Street, one block west of Camino Del Mar, three doors from Stratford Court. He was content with this way of life and even when one of his books became a movie and was nominated for an Academy Award, the elusive author Philip Keenly was conspicuously absent from the gala ceremony.

But now all is not well with Thomas. He has not set a word on the page in three years. Many times he has tried, but it refuses to happen. And so he starts most days sitting in the café surrounded by the jubilant surfers. And this, at least, he enjoys.

Chapter Three

Emelia Falen has a beauty that Thomas Blake adores because it is a clear and perfect beauty of the kind his wife brought to the world. Sitting in the café, Thomas often finds himself staring at Emelia and then, catching himself, he turns and looks away, feigning casual indifference.

Emelia always sits with the other surfers, she herself being a good surfer who can ride a wave like the best of the men. She is tall and svelte with skin the color of creamed coffee—toned that way from the days floating on the sea. She has a lover named Mark, whom everyone calls Gaucho because of his dark hair and his close-cropped beard and because of the jeans and the denim shirts he always wears. Gaucho's eyes are as cool as the morning sky that drapes over the café in the early hours. But inside the café they take on a shade of polished cobalt. His cheeks display pocks that adolescence left him. But this, too, fits well with his gauchoness.

Gaucho and Emelia have been lovers for years. Thomas sees a happiness in Emelia when she is in the café with Gaucho and the other surfers. And on those days when she comes in alone without Gaucho, though happy to be with her friends, it's never the same as when she and Gaucho are there together. Thomas remembers that part of his life with Kathryn.

Every day, while sitting in the café, Thomas vows this will be the day he starts to write again. Many days he has tried. But as the days and the months take over, it seems ever more hopeless.

In the past, he developed countless strategies to get the writing going when it was stalled. His habit was to dive into a mystery, push hard, and keep at it until something emerged that was worth working on. It was a technique he could use to start a new book or prod a stalled one forward.

But now, that approach has failed. Perhaps it is time to abandon the Evan Noir mysteries in favor of something more heartfelt. Something deeper. Something laden with emotion. For years, he has longed to dig into the cathartic inner workings of the mind—to create a piece of literary fiction. Something he never attempted before but now often considers. To extract from his soul all that was ripped from him when Kathryn died. And so, one day after laboring for hours to find the words, he gives up and types, 'Death has no friends', and turns off the computer.

Chapter Four

One morning after Gaucho and the other surfers leave, Emelia approaches Thomas. "I see you here every day," she says.

Thomas looks up and nods.

"You come into our café…here where we gather."

"I like it here," Thomas says. "Do you think maybe it would be better if I went someplace else?"

"Oh no, I don't mean that. It's fine that you're here."

Thomas grants a smile, happy to hear her tell him this. "I see it's mostly just surfers who come to the café," he says.

"Yes…mostly. People gather where they feel they belong, I guess. Of course, it's open to all. It's not a surfer café, not really. It's just that we have kind of taken it over," Emelia says, and laughs a little very gayly.

Thomas likes the cheerfulness of Emelia's voice. It seems true and genuine. "Do you surf every day?" he asks. He knows, of course, that she does. He knows all the surfers do.

"Every day that we can. But we work, Gaucho and I. We both have degrees from UCSD in marine biology, but there are no jobs in that. So, we do what we can to pay the rent and buy food...and drink coffee in the morning at the café and have a beer at night at one of the bars. I work at a boutique on Fifteenth Street." She aims her hand off in the direction. "Gaucho works at a surf shop in Pacific Beach." She waits a moment and says, "Do you surf?"

Thomas shakes his head. "Well...I used to. At one time I did. A little, not very much really. But I haven't done it in a while. Look at me. I must be twice your age. I wouldn't want to embarrass myself," he says.

"You wouldn't," Emelia quickly responds.

"Sometime, I might try again," Thomas allows.

"You should."

"I only think about it. I never do it." He wants to tell Emelia it's like the writing he also never does anymore, and how it embarrasses him to admit—if only to himself—that the words seem lost forever. That he is as unsure with his pen as he is on the crest of a wave. Afraid of tumbling off the board. Falling lopsided backwards and looking silly. Just as he is afraid of writing and then reading the words and hating every one of them. But he is mostly afraid that this is where life has taken him now. He worries that it will never, can never, be better again.

"Why don't you come out? Do you have a board?"

"An old one. A longboard. It's in the garage."

"Some people say those are the best kind...the longboards."

"I've heard that, but it's the only kind I ever used."

"Dust it off and bring it to the water. Come when we're there. We don't chase other surfers away like some groups do. There's room for us all. That's what we believe."

"Room even for a clumsy old man?" he says. He is happy to be talking to Emelia and he hopes she won't have to leave soon, but he knows she probably will.

She looks at her watch. "Yes, even for a clumsy man on a longboard," she replies, getting up. "*Ciao!*"

Thomas stays at the café and looks out the window as the sun captures the sky, dissolving away the mist that filled the cool early air, turning everything clear and bright. He feels good and he knows it is because of the brief conversation with Emelia.

Yes, he often thinks about pulling his surfboard down from the rafters in the garage and trying on the wetsuit he has in a box somewhere up in the attic. He pictures himself teetering on the board, wiping out on a three-foot wave and having to endure the laughter of the young surfers around him. He can give it a try. He can tolerate the laughter and can even laugh at himself. He is good at that. But he wonders whether Emelia was merely being kind to a man who comes into the café and sits alone each day.

There are other cafes in Del Mar and up in Solana Beach and in Cardiff, but he avoids those because they're filled with men and women his age who talk of old things and past years and how life used to be. Although Thomas has plenty to remind him of the past, he tries hard to not let it become his whole life. And so, sitting in the café with the surfers every morning is good for him. For an hour or two, he can be around people who live for the present and the future. Old people think old thoughts, he often tells himself. Young people think young thoughts. He wants to live for the future.

Chapter Five

In the afternoon, Thomas goes for a run along Camino Del Mar from Tenth Street north to the racetrack, then circles down to Torrey Pines and returns home.

Around five o'clock, he ambles down to the railroad tracks that skirt the edge of the low cliffs above the beach. He walks two blocks south along the tracks until he comes to an area near Eighth Street. Sitting on the top of the cliffs, he watches the satin lawn of ocean. A sheet of blue that vanishes far off on the horizon to where a motionless bed of water melds with the sky. In close to shore, as if bullied by the land, the great body of water is rebuffed, forcing it up in swells that topple into rows of whitecaps that barrel over one another in a last defiant act before reaching the soft sand. Out on the ocean, a hundred yards beyond where the water confronts the land, surfers float and dangle and bobble as though riding slow-moving carousel ponies.

Thomas often sits for hours on the cliffs watching the ocean and the surfers. He hasn't been on a surfboard in years. He decides to test his balance. He stands on one leg and then on the other for a long while. He can do this comfortably. His balance is good and he knows his legs are strong from his afternoon runs along the hilly roads and byways of Del Mar and up the high ridges above the ocean. Yet, standing on firm land is far different from balancing on a surfboard perched on undulating ocean waves.

As he watches the cluster of surfers, he wonders if Emelia and Gaucho are among them. Their wetsuits and the far-off distance make it difficult to know for sure.

Returning to his house, Thomas retrieves his surfboard from the rafters in the garage. It's old and it bears evidence of wear—like a well-used guitar that shines with a patina from hands passing across it again and again. Thomas touches the board with the love you would give to that cherished guitar. He sweeps away dust that has settled onto it.

He wonders if Emelia might be right. Perhaps he should take the board down to the water and give it a go. Wait until low tide someday when the waves are small and his chance of a wipeout is minimal. There will be few others out at that time, especially at midday during the week.

He rests the board against the wall and goes inside the house and climbs into the small cubbyhole that is the attic of his bungalow and begins rummaging through boxes in search of his wetsuit. He doesn't remember where he put it, but he feels sure he did not throw it away. Box after box is opened but nothing shows up. Well, all right, perhaps he did throw it in the trash for no reason but to obliterate any memory of that aspect of his life. A certain part of him is forever trying to do that while another part refuses to abide. *Which won out this time*, he wonders, as he pries open boxes, digs through them, and seals them up again.

Standing up, he raps his head hard on the low ceiling. He curses and rubs his head, nearly ready to abandon the search. But he keeps at it and, sure enough, there it is, his old wetsuit, tucked away neatly and safely in the very last box. Climbing down from the attic, he stands in the kitchen and holds the suit in front of him for a moment, then undresses and climbs into it. Frayed at the end of the sleeves, it otherwise still fits, which comes as little surprise given how carefully he watches his diet and sticks to his daily afternoon runs.

In a jocular moment, he crouches down and leans forward, arms poised toward the front of him as though standing deftly on a surfboard while being swept across the sea on a wave. The thought of buying a new wetsuit crosses his mind. Maybe the technology has improved in ways he is unaware of. *Technology always changes, doesn't it?* Consider all the running shoes he allowed himself to purchase in the past several years. Each boasting some new and spectacular benefit for your body and spine and knees. Yet none of them deliver on that promise. So maybe it's best to wear the wetsuit he has and get up on his old surfboard. Then, if all goes well, he can talk himself into new gear.

Chapter Six

Instead of going to the café in the morning, Thomas decides to have coffee in the small but beautiful yard behind his house. The 'Noah' yard he calls it because it has two of everything. Two orange trees, two lemon trees, two avocado trees, two rose bushes, two philodendrons, two bougainvilleas.

He pulls his favorite Evan Noir mystery from the shelf above his desk—each book lined up perfectly first to the last. Eleven in all. He knows right away which to select. *Dark Turning,* the one the critics panned as a retread. No matter what the critics claimed, Thomas felt it bore the richest plot. Dark, yes, but some of the best character development of Evan Noir and his assailants. Noir is up to his elbows in death threats and evilness. Thomas thought the story flowed beautifully; the critics thought it was rubber. The problem, Thomas calculated, was that it had come out too quickly on the heels of a big best seller at a time when his books rolled out effortlessly.

Though he rarely reads more than a page or two from one of his books, when he does, he considers them good but far from perfect. Even throughout the dearth of not writing, he believes he can do better. And yet he worries that he is forever locked out of the process. It is not a good feeling and he hates it.

This is the reason he started going to the café in the morning for coffee. Such a thing he would never do when the words were landing on the page. Morning—quiet and peaceful in the small yard behind his house—is where he worked with only the songs of the mockingbirds and the finches. Instead, for a long time now his mornings are spent at the café, and he knows it is an excuse.

The café is close to where Thomas lives. A mere two blocks up to Twelfth Street and then to Camino Del Mar and around the corner. The surfers come there because it's near the ocean. They surf early in the morning and then climb out of their wetsuits by the cliffs and slip into shorts and T-shirts and flip-flops.

At the café they rest their boards outside next to the windows. Mike, the owner, doesn't mind. He likes them coming to the café. They are well-behaved, usually. And polite, mostly. And their money is good, always. And that's all that matters to Mike.

What's more, Mike is himself a surfer, sometimes even joining the others on the water for an early wave. He has surfed for many years and is good at it, though being late to the sport, he has none of the skills of those who have been on a board from the time they were young. Mike gets along well with Gaucho, and Gaucho thinks Mike is the luckiest man in the world to have such a great café right in the heart of Del Mar.

Sitting in the yard, Thomas pages through *The New York Times* and reads a couple of articles. Politics mostly. Three articles with different twists on how things are going, or not going, in Congress, the White House, the world.

Thomas was once interested in politics. He and Kathryn were passive participants, mostly volunteering for candidates who seemed best-suited to make a positive impact on the world. Thomas could never have been a politician himself. He liked being in the backseat, sitting at a phone bank calling voters, none of the others around him aware they were alongside Philip Keenly—the Evan Noir author. In an age of celebrity, Thomas sought anonymity. He would gush happily when he and Kathryn and Sam Morini, his editor of many years, dined at a posh New York restaurant as Sam bemoaned the faceless bestsellers they were stacking the shelves of the bookstores with. "The public thinks we're making these books up. They think Evan Noir is a creation of some flunky sitting in a backroom office at the publishing house," Sam would tell Thomas, hoping to coax him out of his secret writer's closet. "What a great thing it will be," Sam Morini would surge. "Your book sales will soar from tens of millions to hundreds of millions immediately." Thomas would laugh and deliver a toast with his single malt scotch. Sam knew there was no chance of convincing Thomas to change now.

In the paper, Thomas comes across a book review by

Michiko Kakutani. None of Thomas's books were ever reviewed by her. He is happy of that, given her sharp and sometimes harsh reviews. For that matter, he knows she would never bother with a book like his—straight pulp fiction, detective novels. Kakutani goes for the literary stuff. A new release by Orhan Pamuk or Patrick Modiano, let's say. Now and then, a tell-all by a politician.

Thomas reads through Kakutani's review and wonders again if he might be able to write a book that will take him away from the gum-shoe detectives and into something deeper. He feels he has a book of serious literary fiction lurking inside if only he can bring it out. He knows his mind is still clear, and above all he is thankful for that. Too many people his age are slowly fading away. Or quickly fading away. It is the curse of a society where people live longer and then pay for it with a compromised life. But this is not Thomas's curse. His curse is having the most important person in his life stolen from him and having to live with that day in and day out.

Thomas picks up the copy of *Dark Turning* and reads several pages from the middle of the book. Yes, he can write better, he tells himself. It's easy to see the changes he would make. It's easy to see them once the words are out in print. Like looking at a wave you pass up and then watch it roll to shore, thinking how good it might have been. But he knows this aspect of writing is true for every writer. Those who are worth their salt, at least.

Chapter Seven

Early in the evening, Thomas walks to Fifteenth Street and then over to Maxine's restaurant, an elegant dining spot on the water's edge. He often eats at Maxine's. He feels at home there, having become familiar with the staff and the bartenders.

Thomas knows that Carmine, the hostess, will give him his favorite table, the one that looks broadly out onto the sea and the sky filled with lapsing evening shades of orange and red and ochre and purple.

"Good evening, Mr. Blake," Carmine spryly says. "How good to see you again."

"The name is Thomas," he says and laughs a little, knowing Carmine will never call him Thomas. It doesn't matter; he likes their little game.

"I have a *very* good table for you," Carmine says as if this were Thomas's first ever venture into Maxine's. Thomas knows which table it will be; Carmine frequently keeps it open until late, perchance he shows up. Carmine likes Thomas. She feels kindness toward him. He comes in alone and eats slowly and gazes out at the frothing sea as though caught up in many welcomed new thoughts, or many old and dear memories.

"Yes…I have a good table for you," Carmine happily repeats as she tucks a menu under her arm and leads Thomas through the restaurant. "Everything is delicious tonight. The fish is wonderful and fresh."

Thomas knows that the fish at Maxine's is always wonderful and fresh, and that Carmine will always tell him this as if he were coming into the restaurant for the first time.

"Here's your table." Carmine hands Thomas the menu. "I'll tell Jorge to send over a scotch."

"Ah, that would be wonderful…yes, a single malt, of course. Jorge knows which one." He gives Carmine a grateful wink.

When the scotch arrives, Thomas sits for a long while enjoying the fragrance and the rich flavor of the liquor brimming with the muskiness of peat. It is to be sipped slowly and with care—scotch, the best of all whiskies to Thomas's way of thinking. You must make it last and enjoy every moment. Like time spent with a dear friend.

He looks briefly at the menu and sets it on the table again and returns to the scotch, holding the tumbler as though it were a piece of fine china. He takes a sip and looks out the window to where the last of the sun teeters on the edge of the sea as it falls in with a flare of glitzing light.

Thomas savors the scotch. Even without looking at the menu, he knows what he will have. The Alaskan halibut—always exquisite. Flown in each day and picked up at the dock by a courier from Maxine's.

Thomas is beginning to feel better. Perhaps it's the scotch, or perhaps it is merely being out and away from his house—the first time in several days except for his afternoon runs through Del Mar and down to Torrey Pines and back up the steep hill again. As he sits at the table, he decides he will return to the café in the morning for coffee. He misses being there and he misses the laughter of the surfers.

After eating, Thomas starts through the restaurant when he notices Patrick Simmons sitting at the bar.

"Hey, there," Patrick says, grabbing Thomas's arm. "Here, pull up a stool, buddy."

Thomas likes Patrick. It's good to see him. "In for dinner?" Thomas asks.

"No, I just came from Donarelli's in La Jolla. You know the place, the Italian place. The food there is good, but I needed a drink to finish off the meal." Patrick Simmons flags Jorge.

"Cognac, Jorge," Thomas says. "Pierre Ferrand would be fine."

Jorge nods and presently sets a snifter of warm cognac on the bar.

"Where've you been, old friend?" Patrick Simmons asks. Haven't seen you in weeks."

"Hiding low, I guess," Thomas responds. He thinks about mentioning his visits to the surfer café in the morning but for no special reason decides not to.

"I'm thinking of running the Del Mar to La Jolla next year," Patrick Simmons says. "It won't be for many months yet, next spring in fact."

"It's a good race," Thomas says, he himself having run the legendary half marathon several times.

"A good race and a difficult race. The stretch up the hill at Torrey Pines will kill you," Patrick Simmons says.

Thomas laughs. "Kill you or make you better for having succeeded."

"It will kill you," Patrick Simmons asserts.

"But you'll be happy just the same. How many times have you run it? The race?"

"Six. This will be my seventh."

"Then you'll be fine. Seven is a lucky number."

"Lucky or not, the hill will kill you." Patrick groans despairingly.

Thomas gives the Pierre Ferrand the same care he bestowed upon the scotch. It's good cognac and a suitable finish to an excellent meal. He is glad he ran into Patrick Simmons. Sometimes after dinner Thomas sits at the bar and talks to Jorge, and sometimes if it's near closing time Carmine comes over and has a glass of wine with Thomas and Jorge. But on this night, Thomas is happy to be sharing a drink with his friend.

"I've laid out a plan for the race," Patrick Simmons says. "I want this to be my best time ever."

"If you start preparing now, you'll have no trouble by spring. What are your times?"

"My best is one forty-three," Patrick Simmons says. "I'll never get it down to an hour and a half, that I'm sure of. But under one forty-three will be fine."

"You can do it. You're a strong runner," Thomas says. "Stronger than I am."

"But the hill gets worse every year. I get older and the hill gets higher."

"And every year you turn in a better time than before. See, you're getting younger," Thomas responds. "Not like me. Every year age creeps up on me."

Patrick Simmons moans. "On all of us."

"On me, for sure."

Jorge sets a fresh vodka tonic on the bar. Patrick Simmons stirs it twice, takes a sip, and says, "One forty-three may not be realistic anymore."

"You have months to get ready. If you can hit nine miles comfortably, thirteen point one will be a snap."

Patrick Simmons hopes so.

Thomas crisscrosses his way home from the restaurant. A cool mist floats in from off the ocean. The time spent at Maxine's was enjoyable. He is glad he decided to go there for dinner. He unlocks the door to the house and drops into his favorite living room chair, lights out with only the faint glimmer of a streetlamp shedding a pale glow in through the window. His thoughts turn inward to a dreadful moment, a dreadful day. He recalls everything about it.

人

Rush hour. Kathryn is caught in traffic heading north

on Interstate 805 out of San Diego. Cars bumper to bumper, barely ten feet apart. She grips the steering wheel tightly, glances at the speedometer—seventy-five miles an hour. Cars fly past on her left and right—eight-five, ninety miles an hour. She wants to be home. Had planned to be home by now. At this hour, the sun tricks your eyes. Objects appear and disappear before you can identify them. Quickly on and off the visual radar. A blip on the screen, then gone. What is it? Where did it go? Does it matter?

One mile to the I-5 intersection. The worst stretch of freeway ever created. Twelve horrendous lanes squeeze into six at the pace of a grand prix. Kathryn's hands hold the steering wheel, fingers almost numb. All around are tired drivers. Drivers coming from happy hour. Sober drivers. Pissed-off drivers. Drivers who scream at nobody, at everybody, from behind the windshield. Drivers who, like Kathryn, just want to be home.

A horn rips to her left. Tires screech. Cars spin and smash into a wedge of crunched metal.

Thomas Blake paces the living room. Kathryn should be home by now. No phone call, not a word. He looks out the front window as the sun sinks to the west. The smell of lilacs from the garden. His cell phone rings. He answers.

"Mr. Blake?"

"That's correct."

"You live on Tenth Street…Del Mar?"

"That's correct."

"We need to have you come to the California Highway

Patrol Office at seven one eighty-three Opportunity Road."

"When"

"Now."

"Is everything all right?"

"Can you make it?"

"On my way."

Chapter Eight

Thomas is up as the first light blinks above the hills to the east of Del Mar. He showers, gets dressed, grabs *The New York Times*, and goes to the end of Tenth Street. He watches the frothing sea bubble and churn to shore as he tries to bury away the tormenting thoughts from the night before.

He recalls how thrilled Kathryn was when she read the newest Evan Noir novel fresh from the publisher. How she flashed through it in a single day, two days at the most, talking now and then to Evan as she flipped the pages. Warning him of what she felt was about to happen. Cheering him on while he was in hot pursuit of evilness in whatever form it assumed. And when she finished the book, she would say, "*Oh, Thomas Blake!* You *must* let the world know who the real Philip Keenly is. *You must!*"

Thomas was ready to give up writing. Each of his last two books brought him little excitement. On several occasions he told Kathryn he was getting weary of writing mystery novels. The money from the books kept flowing in, given that nearly every one of the series was still on the shelves in stores throughout the country. The racks at the supermarket checkouts. The airport newsstands.

After Kathryn was gone, Thomas made a vow, more to her than to himself. He will honor her request. He will write one more Evan Noir book, and it will be the best of all. And yet for three years he has been unable to get a word onto the page. Why? If he were to succeed, if he were to write the book Kathryn wanted, would it be an end? Life's final de-nouement? But Kathryn still lives in Thomas's memory, and nothing, no one, can take that from him. Not even his fa-vored creation, Evan Noir.

For many years, writing was Thomas Blake's greatest delight, surpassed only by the happiness Kathryn brought him. Even on the days when he struggled at the keyboard, as agonizing as those times could be, the words would eventu-ally flow. Always, until now.

Thomas feels cheapened for not granting Kathryn her simple wish. He knows perfectly well what he needs to do, and he knows how to do it. It is something that at any other time he could accomplish almost as effortlessly as breathing. He's a writer and he knows how to write. Years ago, he had given Evan Noir life on the pages of his books. Now, Thomas is plodding morosely through life. A flag flapping loosely in a gusty wind. A flag with tattered edges. A flag with faded colors. Kathryn would never approve of this.

Thomas goes to the café as he promised the night be-fore. The surfers are there. Thomas is glad he came back. He thinks briefly about his conversation with Patrick Simmons at Maxine's. He knows he and Patrick are a lot alike, though Patrick has a confidence Thomas has lost.

Thomas sits at one of the small tables and orders coffee and unfurls the copy of the *Times*. The front page is filled with the usual stories. He reads a few paragraphs then pulls the Entertainment section from the middle of the paper. There are several book reviews. He skips them and turns to the third page where he is shocked to see an article with a headline that reads, 'Whatever Happened to Philip Keenly?' Thomas takes a slow sip of coffee and reads the article intently. It's not the first of these provocative pieces about Philip Keenly he's seen. Reading through several paragraphs, he finds nothing that hasn't been rehashed before. His instincts tell him the whole thing is a set-up by his publisher, knowing all the while that Thomas will see the article, hoping it will goad him into turning out another book. Thomas is quite aware that humiliation can be a great motivator in life.

He can almost hear the voice of his editor, Sam Morini, speaking to him through the words in the article. Sam will try every trick to get Thomas to write again. Thomas hates these gimmicks, but he knows that Sam is being pushed by his publisher. That it goes all the way up the food chain. Once, Thomas fell victim to turning in an Evan Noir book that, in Thomas's mind, was not ready for publication. The book sold well, as did all his books, but it failed to meet Thomas's personal high standards. He swore never to get caught in that trap again.

Now, though, it is different. Thomas isn't being nudged

along to wrap up a manuscript that still has a few rough edges. Now, Thomas has no book at all, no manuscript at all—partial or complete. Sam Morini is quite aware of this from the telephone conversations they have every couple of months, the surprise trips Sam makes to Del Mar, claiming to be "…just out in the area visiting one of our new best-selling authors." Thomas would smirk and Sam would grin evasively, trying to hold to the feeble pretext of his visit.

Within little more than half an hour, the surfers begin to leave the café for their day's work. Only Emelia remains. She watches Thomas as he pages through the newspaper. Something of her father, she sees in him. She has been es-tranged from her father for years. They haven't communi-cated since his divorce to Emelia's mother. He remarried. And with that, the relationship between Emelia and her fa-ther ended. He moved on to another wife, another family, and Emelia has no place in that family. That's what Emelia thinks. Or perhaps his second marriage went bad, too, and he can't admit it to Emelia. She wishes she could communi-cate with him, but she doesn't know where he is. She has given up. It hurts.

Emelia senses an inner loneliness in Thomas as he gazes staidly out the window. Whatever is clawing at him, it is right there just below the surface. She gets up and walks over and pulls up a chair. "So, you returned," she jauntily says. "I thought maybe you gave up on our little café."

"No, it's a delight to be here. I used to have coffee in the mornings in the backyard, but that was when I was still…." He almost slips and says writing, but he catches himself. "How's the surfing?" he asks.

Emelia nods. "What kind of work do you do?"

"Once…a lot of work for a big company," Thomas replies. "But now I'm free." He says this as if he's been released from jail. And, yes, many years ago he was released from jail. Released and living freely during the time he spent with Kathryn when his writing was going well. He knew there were no Pulitzer Prizes for fiction, no Nobel Prizes for Literature, awaiting him. He knew there never would be, and it was fine with him. So long as he wrote pulp fiction he could hide away from all the glitter that would go with those accolades.

"Gaucho and I like our jobs. We could work some place else…I suppose. But we prefer the freedom, the chance to be out on the water every day."

"That's good, you're lucky," Thomas says. "Lucky that you already know what you want and don't want."

"Yes, but someday this will probably change," Emelia says, somewhat sadly.

"It might. But that doesn't matter. For now, you know what you want."

"Gaucho's grandfather tells us we all change over time. Sort of like the waves as they roll across the sea minute by minute. He was drafted and sent to Vietnam when he was nineteen, and when he got back he swore he would work to change the world. And then he got a good job and nothing he did changed anything. That's what he says. He tells me

I'm idealistic. That Gaucho and I are both idealistic. He says this will change one day and we'll become just like everyone else. He always laughs when he tells me that. But it makes me sad to think it might happen."

"In life, you have to stay true to what you believe in. It isn't easy though."

"We know what we believe in, and we plan to stay true to it," Emelia affirms, and then says, "So tell me, are you planning to join us out on the water? Did you dig out your wetsuit and board yet?"

Thomas confesses he did.

Emelia is delighted. "That's terrific. You can come out with us whenever you want. We'll save a good wave for you."

This causes Thomas to laugh. "The one you save for me will be the one you waste for yourself."

"The sea has lots of good waves," Emelia gleams. She looks at her watch. "Oh, lord. I have to go." Getting up to leave, she turns and says, "By the way, next week some of us are going down to Ensenada on the coast in Baja. Have you ever been there?"

"Oh, sure…now and then. But I haven't been there in quite a while."

"Perfect. Then you can come with us."

Thomas is stunned. "You're kidding. What will the others say…who else is going?"

"Gaucho and me and a fellow named Lenny…Lenny Stark. And his girlfriend, Margo. They're fun people. You'll like them."

Thomas shakes his head. "I don't think so. They won't want me tagging along." He looks at the newspaper resting on the table, then looks at Emelia. "Well, it's nice of you to invite me," he says, "but I doubt that I'll go."

"Well…give it thought." With a "*Ciao*," Emilia is gone.

After Emelia leaves, Thomas sits for a while mulling over her offer to join them on the trip to Baja. *It might be fun*, he thinks. But he worries the others will have a problem with him coming along. *What in the world was she thinking to suggest such a thing?*

Chapter Nine

The sky is bright and clear and the day is warm. Thomas checks for low tide in the newspaper—two in the afternoon. A more perfect time there could not be. He puts on his wetsuit. Surfboard under arm, he starts down Tenth Street toward the aqua blue Pacific and turns along the railroad tracks until he reaches the narrow path that curves its way to the beach.

Thomas sets his surfboard on the sand and looks over the ocean. Everything is fine. The waves are low. Barely three feet, if that. They roll to shore smooth and steady until, as they near the beach, they flip into small white ridges. Now, even at low tide, Thomas is not sure this is such a great idea. Looking at the water, he begins to rethink it.

He zips up his wetsuit and grabs the board and walks slowly and determinedly to the water's edge and wades in. He stands knee-deep for a second, then plows into the water and slides onto the board and paddles out onto the smooth and silky sea, feeling a surge of courage gradually well up inside him. A small dose of courage, yes, but enough to keep him from retreating to shore.

Thomas floats just beyond where the waves are breaking. If a good one comes along, he will ride it and climb to his feet and, who knows, maybe merely topple awkwardly off the board. Fifteen minutes pass and he has yet to take a wave. He watches many good ones sneak past him. "Ah, damn, there it goes!" he whispers to himself and the sea, though he knows a million more good waves are still to come.

Then he sees it. He watches as it approaches silently behind him—keeping an eye on it as it rises above the unbroken platform of open water. At just the right second before it reaches him, he starts paddling. On the edge of the wave, he climbs on his board and lets it carry him toward shore until, tilting too far back, he falls sideways off the board. He rises from the water and laughs and cheers his performance.

Even in failure, it was a success. A small success, indeed, but enough to quell all his unwarranted fears. Just enough to make him lie on the board and paddle out again and wait—straddling the board—for another wave. He wants a bigger one now. He watches as they rise synchronously one after another. Soon, a good one will crest up. That's always how it is. Whether at low tide or high tide. *There, there it is...yes!* Thomas watches, calculates carefully as it approaches. At the perfect moment, he climbs on the board and zips across the edge of the wave as it turns into bubbling white foam. He rides it all the way in without a fall. Standing in the shallow water, he shakes his arms joyously in the air like an Olympian. It feels good.

Thomas stays on the water for half an hour, taking wave after wave until his face tingles from the chill of the sea. He hobbles out and sits on the sand and lets the sun bake him. He is glad Emelia prodded him into digging his wetsuit from the attic and his board from the garage.

Thomas's first attempt on the board went well. He is pleased with his performance. He might even be able to get out on the water with the surfers from the café, though he only needs to watch the boys down the beach to his left—as they zip and dart across the waves on their shortboards—to realize he will never be like that. It doesn't bother him. He is not trying to relive his youth. Not trying to get back time that cannot be recaptured. Rather, Thomas is haunted by the silent awareness that, in a world where youthfulness permeates everything, his life—like an ebbing tide—is slipping away.

Chapter Ten

The next morning, Thomas walks to the edge of the cliff above the beach. He is lifted by the humble experience of the time spent with his surfboard the day before. He watches a lone runner passing across the beach at the boundary of the water. Thomas can almost make out Patrick Simmons from the forward-charging running style.

The afternoon brings low winds and a satin sky. Seeing Patrick Simmons chugging down the beach so determinedly earlier in the day prompts Thomas to give serious consideration to the Del Mar to La Jolla Half Marathon that is soon approaching. He changes into his running clothes and starts for the front door. Opening it, there on the porch, like an ephemeral apparition, is his editor, Sam Morini.

"Thomas!" Sam bursts, smiling gleefully. "Whad'ya know, I was just getting ready to ring the bell."

Thomas can't help but laugh. He shakes Sam's hand and invites him in. The contrast in appearances between the two is stark. Sam, blanched and parched by the cold wind that explodes down Fifth Avenue in the winter, looks as white as a blank sheet of paper. Thomas's face holds the glow of a tan one acquires living year-round in Southern California.

Sam starts barking out words. "Look at you," he says, stepping into the house. "Why you're the picture of health. I was up in LA today visiting a gal we just signed on. Wait till you see her stuff! Just wait! Let me tell you, she's good, real good! And I *had* to come down and see how my favorite of all writers is doing…see what he's up to," Sam Morini says, standing in the living room wearing an expensive polo shirt and chinos and deck shoes, all brand new, trying to appear casual.

"So you decided to zip down the road and pay a visit to old Thomas Blake, is that it?"

"Good a reason as any to be here, don't you think?" Sam says, with a fist bump to Thomas's shoulder.

"Come now, I know your routine, Sam. Surely, you don't think I've forgotten how you operate," Thomas chides.

"Ha, ha," Sam chortles. A second fist bump to Thomas. "Hell no, truth is I feared you fell off the face of the planet out here. Something like that. Then too, a little warm Southern California sunshine can't hurt a bit, winter being as god-awful cold as it is this year."

They sit in the living room. The streak of yellow sunlight coming in through the west facing window spreads out a sheet of warmth.

Sam Morini wastes no time in getting to the matter at hand, despite a fraudulent effort to deke his way around the issue. "Well, Thomas," he says in a low bark. "Tell me, where is Evan Noir these days? If I know you, and I think I do pretty well, I'd bet our old friend Evan is nearing the end of yet another cliffhanger." He waits and watches surreptitiously for Thomas's reaction. If Sam Morini is good at anything, it is reading body language.

Thomas doesn't address the question. Instead, he brings up the article about Philip Keenly that appeared in *The New York Times*. He leans back in his chair and clasps his hands behind his head. "You didn't by any chance have something to do with it, did you?" Thomas says.

Sam Morini puckers his lips and looks unconvincingly confused, brow furrowed. "Oh, *thaaat!*" he says. "*Now* I know what you're talking about. I saw the article." He leans on his elbow and rubs his hands together as if attempting to find an explanation that will suit both of them. "Well, you can say one thing for sure, there's a whole world out there that's chomping at the bit, waiting for another Evan Noir mystery. Christ almighty, Thomas, it's been so long since the last one. Another Evan Noir will fly off the shelves in the stores. Hell's bells, it'll hit the top of *The New York Times* best seller list instantly...Amazon too." He makes a gesture like a rocket blasting off. "Right to the top. That's what it'll do. Straight up!"

Sam Morini isn't telling Thomas anything he doesn't already know. Yes, it probably would soar to the top of the lists like a rocket, just as Sam suggests.

Sam breathes deeply and exhales. His voice turns contrite, his tone lower. The barking is gone. "I'm not going to lie about it, Thomas," he says. "If nothing else, all these years we've had absolute total trust in each other...wouldn't you say? Yes, of course we were behind the article in the *Times*. Pure publicity. You know what I mean. But I'm just an editor. I don't make those kinds of calls. The clowns in advertising and publicity do. Those jocks do. They come up with these schemes. And, of course, the *Times* was complicit. They knew all along what was going on. They knew lots of people would read the article. That's all that matters to them. The readers."

Thomas slumps in the chair while Sam rambles through his explanation. Truth is, Thomas has no problem with the publisher's little cabal of trickery. He's grateful they still have confidence in him. They could have cut him loose...could have viewed him as washed up and let him go. But they didn't.

"Yes, I did come out here to see if I can help with the writing...stuff," Sam confesses. "Why be evasive," he adds, rearranging the collar of his shirt.

Thomas huffs softly. He starts to speak, backs off, and gloomily says, "You know how it's been, Sam. I know you do."

"Dry?"

"Like the Mojave. Worse, even."

"All of our writer's go through that sooner or later."

Thomas never talks about this with anyone. How can he? Only a handful of people know he's the real author of the Evan Noir books, not Philip Keenly. Just Sam Morini and a small collection of others at the publishing house know he writes books at all. They keep the lid on it like it's the code of the nuclear arsenal. Yet, Sam Morini is well aware that Thomas's problem came about after Kathryn's death. Sam wants to help, but he doesn't know how. He's a damn good editor, but a piss-poor psychiatrist. He's a friend, a colleague, a cheerleader for Thomas. Sam has an inner empathy that goes beyond the obligation of his job. He likes and respects and worries about Thomas. Likes and respects and, yes, *worries* about him. They've been close friends throughout most of Thomas's writing career. Sam never approved of Thomas hiding out as the ghost writer of the Evan Noir mysteries, but he's learned to live with it. He abides it.

Sam likes for his authors to make the rounds on the talk shows and radio shows when they have a new book. The evening comedy shows and the afternoon shows. Oprah. What's more, Thomas Blake—with his clear blue eyes that seem to hold all the secrets of the world behind them, his even and strong jaw, his ideal blend of black and silver hair—cuts the perfect image as the author of a hard-boiled tough guy like Evan Noir. Just to look at Thomas Blake makes you want to buy one of his mysteries.

Sam Morini knows that Kathryn was the ideal soulmate for Thomas. They had no children. Their lives centered around each other. There were times when Sam felt that Thomas would walk away from his writing, never to return, if it meant choosing between the writing and Kathryn. But Thomas was never confronted with that because whatever he wanted, Kathryn wanted. And whatever Kathryn wanted, he wanted. Absolute synergy.

Now, Sam has come to visit Thomas with the hope of helping him. He worries about Thomas's health even though Thomas sparkles like the image of perfect health. But then that can be said for a good ninety percent of everyone Sam passes in Del Mar, no matter what their inner condition.

Thomas says, "You must accept, we must accept...better yet, *I* must accept that there are no more books coming from the typewriter of Thomas Blake. And if that's the case, how terrible is it?"

"Is that true or are you just thinking out loud?" Sam asks.

"It's very possible," Thomas replies, quickly, coldly.

"Let's try this. What if you were to get away for a while? A nice long trip. Italy, perhaps. Or Paris. Have you considered that? Or a cruise somewhere. One of those very long ones that go to exotic places. Something really different."

Thomas doesn't answer. He merely shakes his head.

"I know you think it's crazy, but I've seen how those things can help. It did for my brother when he was in a similar situation," Sam says. His hand comes up and mechanically repositions his collar again. It seems to be something he has incorporated into his daily routine, whether sitting at his desk in New York or sitting in Thomas's living room.

Thomas imagines himself in Italy—in Florence, let's say—all by himself, carrying with him the memory of Kathryn. Or in one of the other places they had planned on visiting. The places that were on their bucket list should the time arrive. Budapest, for example. Exactly why Budapest, they weren't sure, but it had made it up near the top of the list. They had heard good things about it. Prague, too. Or a long trek across Russia on the Trans-Siberian Railway. Those were all part of the bucket list entries they had made. Those lists that work great in movies but never do so well in real life.

"Get-away trips like that do nothing for me," Thomas says. "I tried a few. Not like you suggest maybe, but others like them. They only serve to amplify the whole matter in my mind."

"I'm just trying to help. You know that."

"I've given it a lot of thought, believe me I have. The writing and all, I mean. And maybe there is no more coming from me because there isn't meant to be any more. And it's not about the bucks, the money I mean. I'm well set with that. The reason there's no more is because I'm used up. Spent. Done. Finished as a writer. Let's just be honest about it."

"It's not just the writing I'm worried about. It's the inner sense of...of self-worth. How are you doing on that, if I can pry a bit."

"You should stick to being an editor. You're a hell of a bad shrink."

"Sometimes I'm a hell of a bad editor, too," Sam says, with genuine sincerity.

"I think you got the editor thing pegged pretty well. But you're still a hell of a bad shrink."

Sam rubs his palm through the short bristles of hair that poke straight up on the top of his head.

"If I never wrote another word, would it matter to anyone? Would it...really?"

"It would matter to a whole *lot* of folks, Thomas. You're right, I am a hell of a lousy shrink, but I know the publishing industry. It would matter to a hell of a lot of readers. People love your stuff."

"You know, of course, this crap we do, the writing I mean, it doesn't just fill the pages all by itself."

"I almost wish it did," Sam groans. "All right. Plan B. What if you come to New York for a while? Get a place on the East Side. You know what the energy is like in New York. It can be infectious. I know life here is pretty damn idyllic. Oh yes, pretty damn idyllic. I mean, look at me, look how I'm dressed and it's practically the middle of winter..."

"It *is* the middle of winter," Thomas corrects.

"Yes, my point exactly. It's the middle of winter and here I am in khakis and a polo shirt...khakis and a polo shirt! I'm dressed like it's July. Back in New York the snow is stacked up to my balls. Last week I slipped on a patch of ice and nearly busted my goddamn ass. But pretty soon it'll be spring and then summer, and New York comes alive in the summer. Absolutely alive!"

"Yes, you're a hell of a bad shrink, Sam," Thomas repeats. He looks at the ceiling and thinks for a moment. Sam's words do resonate, but Thomas is not prepared to admit it.

"Well, I'm going to be in town for a while. Staying down

in La Jolla at the Hotel Valencia. Maybe even put on the old running shoes and take off down the beach or somewhere. Get some sun, too. Fill up the old vitamin D tank and all. Isn't that what they claim, the docs, we get vitamin D from sunlight? Don't understand how that can be. I always thought we get vitamins from vegetables...or One-A-Day tablets. But then, what do I know?"

"Ten, fifteen minutes a day...no sunscreen. But after that, get out the SPF 30 if you're outside. Skin cancer is a real killer."

"You should come down to La Jolla, Thomas. We'll have a drink or get something to eat. Or maybe I'll come up here. What do you say?"

"No talk of trips to Italy or France or long cruises?"

"Nah, none of that," Sam says, warmly. The barking is gone. His voice, full of gentle benevolence.

Chapter Eleven

One evening while they are making dinner, Emelia tells Gaucho she had invited Thomas to join them in Ensenada. Gaucho looks at her like she's crazy. Why in the world would she do that? Sure, Gaucho has seen Thomas sitting off by himself at the café, and he remembers Emelia once saying she feels sorry for him, that he seems to have no friends, and that he somehow reminds her of her father who pulled himself out of Emelia's life and refuses to let her in. But Gaucho has his doubts about Emelia's idea. What will Thomas do in Ensenada? They're going there to surf and, of course, to go into town at night and drink beer and tequila at Hussong's, the bar that all gringos go to in Ensenada.

"He can come to Hussong's with us, if he wants. Or he can stay at the camp on the beach, if he wants," Emelia says, referring to their way of saving the cost of a motel.

"And we have to consider Lenny and Margo. What will they think about this?" Gaucho says.

Emelia and Gaucho met Lenny and Margo down on the beach one day soon after they moved to San Diego from Minnesota. They became good friends and did many things together as a group of four. Barely a day passes that Margo doesn't vow never to live in Minnesota again. She loves the eternal warmth of Southern California. The energy. The lifestyle. Lenny and Margo first climbed on a surfboard riding the roiling waves on Lake Superior. But the grey water and grey sky held none of the allure that comes from being out on the glistening azure-blue Pacific.

"Margo can't go," Emelia says. "She has some big project the company wants her to finish."

"Okay, Lenny then. What about him?"

"I think he'll be okay with it. Nothing bothers Lenny...or Margo for that matter. They have a Midwest sort of attitude."

"Have you asked Lenny if it's all right?"

"Not yet, but I think it will be fine."

"Well, you need to ask him," Gaucho insists.

"Of course. I will."

"Yes. We can't do this without everyone approving."

"I'll mention it to him. I will."

"As soon as possible or the trip may be off if you wait too long."

"Tomorrow at the café, I'll bring it up. If Lenny doesn't like the idea, then we go without Thomas. It doesn't matter whether he comes along or not. I just thought it would be fun for him. That he would enjoy it."

"Cripes, he's as old as my father, probably," Gaucho says.

"I know, but he's different. He seems sad inside."

"Lots of people are sad inside."

"Of course, but even so he hasn't lost his outlook on life. That's what I see. I talked to him a couple of times at the café. He has a...what should I say, an inner tug-of-war going on. Many people his age do, I think."

"Many people our age do," Gaucho says.

"I think he'll do fine in Ensenada. He's very healthy...do you know he runs every day, and he even used to surf but he hasn't done it in some years now."

"Yeah, well, tomorrow at the café check with Lenny."

"I will."

Part II

Chapter One

The two-car caravan leaves Del Mar at mid-morning. Thomas rides with Gaucho and Emelia in Gaucho's vintage Land Cruiser. Lenny follows behind in his truck.

Crossing the border into Mexico goes smoothly. In no time they are rolling down Highway 1 past Tijuana along the western skirt of Baja. Salty sea air doctored with smells of Mexico blows in through the window. Musty fragrances of dry hot earth. Luscious scents of food from kitchens. Thomas loves the smells. When he traveled to Mexico with Kathryn, he was always struck by how sterile and odorless the US seemed, and how the air in Mexico was so vibrant and full of life.

They pull off the road south of Ensenada along a stretch of open beach near a cluster of palms. Gaucho had told Thomas to bring a tent, they always camp on the beach. Thomas unfolds a small tent. One good enough to keep out the tormenting nighttime venturings of insects, mosquitoes, snakes, tarantulas, scorpions, and all other kind of roaming vermin. Mosquito netting across the front and back gives the breeze free reign to come and go. Gaucho and Emelia have a tent. Lenny has one for himself.

No sooner are the tents up than the four are on the water. Thomas Blake, the last one out, paddles slowly if perhaps a little dutifully behind the other three.

The waves are more intimidating than anything Thomas has been on in years. Though the others wait for a large ripe wave, Thomas hopes for something less feral for his first attempt. One after another, each of the three takes a wave. Gaucho, then Emelia, then Lenny. Thomas watches as they slide deftly across the breaking surf just under the curling tip of foaming water. Now, Thomas will need to muster all the courage he can draw upon. He looks behind him. He will wait for a good wave—one to his liking. He sees it coming. Heaving up from the sea in a quiet slow rise.

He glances at the shore where the others are standing knee-deep in water, boards under arm, waiting for Thomas to get a wave. It grows up higher and higher. Thomas starts paddling, calling to it and saying, "You are mine. Do me well and I will do you well." At the perfect second, as the wave rises, he climbs on his board. Crouching and angling and zig-zagging—hair thrown back by the blast of air in his face—he heads to shore.

He hears the rustling of the thick water below him. He might even hear Gaucho cheering him on, but all of Thomas's attention is now on the wave that curls into a hollow cone to his right. A moment of total communion with the sea. *Get ready*, he tells himself. *If this beast flips me, I'll roll and avoid the sharp bottom of the sea and come up with a smile. But if it doesn't*.... He soars across the crest until it breaks humbly into nothing in the shallow water.

For four hours, they repeat this. Numbed and chilled by the water, Thomas lumbers to shore and falls spread-eagle on the sand. Momentarily, the others come in and stand over him and laugh.

Later, as the sun folds onto the water in a grand tapestry of flaming shades of pink and red and purple, Gaucho recovers fins and mask and snorkel and a speargun from the Land Cruiser. He heads to the sea and swims out to the clear water beyond where the waves are breaking. In less than half an hour, he returns with two red snapper that he cleans and fillets. Lenny builds a fire and Emelia starts a pot of rice dosed with jalapeno and onion and tomato.

"Pops did great out there on the water today," Gaucho says, giving Thomas a nod. "How did it feel?"

"Whew! Total rush."

Gaucho heats a pan and drops a dab of butter and a squirt of lemon into it. The fillets spatter and crackle as he sets them in one by one.

Lenny pulls beer from the ice chest and tosses one to each in the group. "I feel great, but by this time tomorrow, I'll feel better yet. It takes me a whole day to unwind. Being in Mexico with nothing but the surf and sea clears my head of all the crap that's going on back in the states. For a little while at least I think about nothing but being here."

Emelia looks at Thomas. "Have you been to Hussong's? Hussong's Cantina?" she asks.

"Hussong's? If I remember, yes. Sometime a while ago, I think."

"It's a gringo bar in Ensenada. Ensenada is filled with all kinds of bars, but Hussong's is the place where most people go. A tourist trap, to be sure, but a fun tourist trap just the same."

Lenny groans. "It'll be fine so long as I don't hit the tequila. That stuff'll destroy you."

Gaucho says, "I heard it's good for the heart. That's what they say."

"Ha...good for the heart maybe, but not the brain," Emelia says.

A book rests on a towel next to Lenny.

"What are you reading?" Thomas asks.

Lenny tosses the book to him.

Thomas tries not to laugh. On the cover is:

Cold Blooded Killer
An Evan Noir Mystery
by
Philip Keenly

"Ever read stuff by this guy?" Lenny says.

"Uh...not sure. Might have," Thomas takes a sip of beer and lets it wash through his mouth.

"Well, I've probably read them all," Lenny says. "For a while, this Keenly fellow was turning out books like linked sausages, but then he suddenly quit. Sorta too bad is how I see it."

Thomas pages indifferently through the book as if it's new to him.

"Nothing ever about Keenly…strange," Lenny says. "I tried to hunt him up on the internet once. Got nada."

"So, Evan Noir, is that it?" Thomas says, reading the back cover.

"Gumshoe. Hardboiled detective. All Keenly's books are about him…Evan Noir. I like this kind of stuff. I can fly through it in no time. Probably will finish it before we leave here."

Thomas hands the book back to Lenny, who sets it on the towel with elemental care.

"Keenly hasn't published a thing in a while now," Lenny says.

Thomas knows this to be all too true. It's been almost five years since the last Evan Noir book. A genuinely long spate of time given that the other books hit the stores religiously barely two years apart. Just when one began to fade from *The New York Times* best seller list, another rose to take its place. Thomas Blake could turn out an entire novel—a hundred and twenty thousand words, more sometimes—in ten months. Twelve at the most. But that was then.

"Personally, I think he croaked, that's what I think," Lenny continues. "Croaked and the publisher doesn't want the world to know it. They want his fans to think there's still another book just around the corner."

Emelia chips in. "Well, I read that some people think

Keenly never existed at *all*. That he's a creation of the publisher, and that the books are written by a bunch of people there. I saw an article like that in *The LA Times* once. It's all very strange."

Thomas Blake listens—it isn't the first time he's heard banter like this about one of his books.

Lenny says, "I'll tell you this much, I'd give anything to be cranking out books like Keenly. Wow, wouldn't that be a gas! You know this Keenly guy is rolling in bucks. You can be sure of that. I'll bet he lives in some big gigantic mansion somewhere and no one knows he's the dude writing all the books. You know, when I was in college in Minnesota, I wanted to be a writer. Still think about it from time to time. I worked for the school newspaper for a couple of years pumping out dumb little articles. I had plans to write novels…great big novels. Christ, imagine how much fun it would be to do what Keenly does…or did." Lenny thinks about that for a second. He takes a long slow sip of beer. "Anyway, here's what *I'd* do. After I had a couple of big bestsellers, you know of the kind Keenly's had, I'd get a house in La Jolla. One of those real beauts on the hill that looks down onto the ocean. A house with a wall of windows that face west so I could open them in the morning to let the sea breeze in. I'd write all morning and then every afternoon I'd head down to be beach to ride a wave." He rolls his eyes in delight.

"Would you be like Keenly and hide your identity?" Thomas Blake asks, curious to hear what Lenny will say.

Lenny doesn't think for long before replying, "Hell no! Why do that?"

"And every day when you go to the beach, someone comes up to you with a book and a pen and asks you to sign it," Thomas says.

"Of course they will, but that's not so bad."

"And they come to your door and do the same thing...day after day."

Lenny thinks, this time a little longer. "Possibly," he says.

"And they come up to you in a restaurant and—"

"And in the café, too," Emelia says. "If you go to a café like ours to have a cup of coffee, let's say. To read the newspaper maybe."

"I don't think someone as famous as Philip Keenly would spend his time in a surfer café," Lenny proclaims.

"It would be the best place because no one would expect you to be there," Thomas Blake replies. But Thomas is more interested in finding out if Lenny has done any writing. "Have you started a novel yet?"

"Nah...just a couple of stupid short stories, that's all. The problem is if I got real serious about it, I'd have to give up my day job and spend all my time writing. And I guarantee, I'd *starve*."

"Oh, I don't know. Thomas thinks everyone should stick to their goals no matter what," Emelia says. "That's what he told me."

"Well, I could have done a better job of it, too,"

Thomas says, in an empty tone. "We all can, I guess. Dreams are easy to imagine but hard to live by."

"Did you live up to yours?" Lenny asks.

Thomas shrugs and thinks for a second. "Did I? I guess so. I don't know, I think I did…maybe."

"Well, dreams can be damn hard to live up to," Gaucho says. "That I know for sure. We exist in a world where everything is moving faster and faster, and some days I want it all to just slow down a little. That's why it's good to be out on the water. The waves come in just like they did yesterday and just like they'll do tomorrow. Not faster, not slower. Life can speed up, but the waves will be the same. I like the consistency of that. The one thing that no one can ever change."

"You can be sure there are people on this planet who *would* change it if they could…just to screw with you," Lenny says.

"But they *can't*, no matter how hard they try," Gaucho says.

"They'll try. You just wait," Lenny half-heartedly insists.

"And they'll fail," Gaucho declares in a voice of determined assurance.

"They may not try to change the flow of the waves. Not intentionally maybe, but a lot could happen unintentionally," Emelia says. "Look at what's going on with the planet today. If you mess with it enough, things change—even the oceans. Sure, the waves will still be out there, and the ocean may look the same, but it'll be different. Fish will die and the higher temperatures will melt the polar caps and the shoreline will move farther inland. It's already happening. Many people around the globe know this. But in the US, a lot of people are in denial. It's like when Galileo said the sun, not the Earth, is the center of the solar system. The Popes refused to believe him and dragged him before the Inquisition."

Dinner is good—fish and rice, birotes and tortillas that they bought at the market in Ensenada on the way to the beach. The air is beginning to cool as the sea breeze blows quietly through the camp.

Chapter Two

Hussong's has changed little since 1892 when the German immigrant Johann Hussong opened the doors to the bar. Happily lit inside, it is filled with a charity of liveliness and chatter and laughter. The four move through the cantina and take a table in the corner away from the traffic. Gaucho orders beer for the group.

Thomas Blake's memories of Hussong's are beginning to come back. He was there with Kathryn when they were on their way to Cabo San Lucas to celebrate the publication of a book. He isn't sure which one—his sixth or seventh. Might have been his eighth. It doesn't matter. The memory of Kathryn fills Thomas's thoughts as he looks around the cantina. He can almost recall the table where they sat. The light as it crept in through the open door and the tarnished windows. The smell of the cantina—enchiladas, tacos, guacamole, the toasted tortilla chips and salsa, the pico de gallo. Kathryn's bubbly laughter and merry smile.

When the beer arrives, Gaucho gives a toast to Thomas Blake's success on Ensenada's tubular waves. Thomas raises his beer cheerfully. A waitress sets a bowl of salsa and tortilla chips on the table. Thomas ladles a chip through the salsa.

"But I'd be a damned liar if I said I wasn't a little spooked by the waves today. I haven't been on anything like that in years," Thomas says.

"They're bigger here, all right," Lenny says. "The first time Margo and I came down with Gaucho and Emelia, I thought there was no way I could get on one of those. But I did, just like you did. And it felt great."

"So later tonight we'll celebrate. A margarita perhaps," Thomas Blake says. "I heard it was invented here, the margarita...that's what I heard. Right here at Hussong's. We'll have a margarita to celebrate today's success."

"Better than doing shooters of tequila and then wobble out of here and try to find our way down the highway to our camp," Emelia says.

Thomas Blake is happy to be sitting with the group in Hussong's, yet it seems like everywhere he goes, his thoughts of Kathryn are never far off, as deep and rich as ever. The picture of her in his mind is precise and sharp, vivid. At times he wishes he could store the memory of her away in a sacred little place that he can go to just when he wants to. Yet, Thomas Blake's thoughts of Kathryn remain as true as anything that exists today. The psyche of a writer—the capacity to take a rough and formless piece of clay and shape and mold and trim it until a character, real to life, emerges. Or to sustain the past, living forever in him.

The cantina becomes lively and boisterous. Gringos and Mexicans sing as the mariachis wail and croon while edging their way through the tight spaces between the tables, carrying guitars and horns, wearing dazzling black and white and red uniforms. Sombrero big as a duck pond.

When the drinks arrive, another toast is given. "Salud," Emelia says.

The glasses clank. "Salud."

Chapter Three

Thomas Blake is up well before the others. The morning is blissful—the sky, clear and dotted with fragile silky clouds. Thomas puts on a T-shirt and shorts and takes off barefoot, tracing the rim of the water. The waves roll in slow and perpetual, almost silently. Pushing their way inch by inch up the sand as the day moves toward high tide that will peak in the afternoon.

Thomas picks up shells as he saunters along, inspecting each one and delivering them back into the surf. One is particularly beautiful. It has fine colors of blue and purple. After studying it for several minutes, he quietly declares, "Ah, ha! This will be my lucky shell! Lucky for what, I don't know, but it will be lucky just the same." He slips it into his pocket.

Far down the beach, he can barely make out the tents in the distance behind him. He stops and sits on the sand and looks onto the water to where the fog from the sea is held captive above the blue-green ocean. He feels the warmth of the sun as it slips across Baja, eager to display itself over the broad and endless Pacific.

Thomas sits on the beach for half an hour, perhaps

longer, thinking the recurrent thoughts that perpetually haunt him. Off to his right, he sees someone ambling down the beach in his direction and realizes it is Emelia. She stops and picks up shells much as Thomas did. Glancing ahead, she sees Thomas. Her step quickens.

"Well, look who I find out here so early in the morning," she says as she approaches. She sits on the sand next to Thomas.

"It's a terrific morning," Thomas says.

"Gorgeous. And the day will be hot. You can feel the sun already and it's barely over the top of the peninsula."

"It feels good. It helps me shake off the effects of the drinks from last night. A quick visit to the water would help even more, but I have no intention of that. I'm not good at self-inflicted pain."

"It would help clear the head."

Thomas agrees, but only in spirit.

Emelia scoops small handfuls of sand and filters them through her fingers, building little three-inch stacks and mounds. "Hussong's was lively last night. Don't you think?"

Thomas nods. He leans back and stretches.

"It's so quiet out here. Isn't it?" Emelia says softly, as if not to disturb the silence. "It's moments like this that I think a lot about my father. During the quiet times like now the thoughts of him come back to me."

Then she tells Thomas about a queer recurrent dream she has every couple of weeks. She is three possibly four years old and her father is pushing her on a swing in a park.

She is happy and filled with joy. She can hear him behind her singing something. Hear him singing but, strangely, she cannot make out the words. Just the melody of the words, whatever they are, as they rise and fall. It's a bubbly song and it fills the air as she stretches out her legs and points her toes straight ahead and tilts far back on the swing—and soars through the air.

"I don't know if that ever happened," Emelia says. "I don't remember that it did, not like in the dream, at least. But it must have or I wouldn't keep having the dream. Don't you think? It's a happy dream...happy because I'm with my father. But it's a sad dream, too. Sad because it's a time from my past." Emelia stops dripping the sand through her fingers and looks at the churning water for a moment, then digs softly through the tiny pebbles once more. "On those days after I've had this dream, my father, his presence...or lack of it," she says, in a quiet sauterne voice. "Well, on those days I feel as though he's still nearby. As if I might pass him during the day on the street in Del Mar or La Jolla or someplace. And I imagine he will stop and look at me in surprise, that he will recognize me instantly." She quits building sand castles and looks at Thomas. With a fragile smile, she says, "So there you have it, Brother Thomas...my confession."

"We all carry with us things we can't change, I suppose," Thomas says, disconsolately. "Things that are far beyond our grasp. I know how you feel. It's like the sea mist. You can feel it on your face. You can smell it. But you can't reach out and grab it. Even if you want to."

"And yet we want to, don't we? The lost memories we have, I mean. They are like the sea mist, as you say. We want to grasp them. To hold them. To not let them get away. That's how I feel when I think about my father. But like the mist that vanishes before us, my father left too. I still keep thinking he'll show up someday when I walk through Del Mar or when I run an errand on my lunch hour. I imagine that he'll pass me, like I just described, and that he'll be over-joyed to see me." Emelia stops speaking. The warmth of the sun holds the moment in a calm and reassuring way. After a while she says, "But each day I know that won't happen. I have to be realistic. Not pretend something will happen when I know it won't."

"You can't be sure," Thomas says. "He may one day feel the need to reach you."

"So, tell me, Brother Thomas, are you happy you came with us on our trip to Ensenada?"

"It's been perfect. Just what I needed."

"A chance to get away from Del Mar?"

"Even a place like Del Mar, as nice as it is, yes. It's always good to get away now and then. I don't do that very often anymore. Should, but I don't. And I would never come down here and put a tent on the beach by myself. It might be fun, I suppose…perhaps. But—"

"Lonely?"

Thomas nods. "But, you know, I still worry that Gaucho and Lenny might think I'm a pest. That I'm—"

"No, never. I know Gaucho very well. When he says

he's fine with something, he means it. Gaucho is like that. He's been my whole life for a long time now. I know him like I know the palm of my hand. And Lenny? What can you say about Lenny? He's your regular go-along-to-get-along sort of guy. Nothing bothers Lenny. It must be some Midwest thing—a Minnesota thing. I don't know. I've never been to Minnesota. But if everyone there is like Lenny, it must be a nice place. Here in Southern California, people don't always say what they're really thinking. Lenny is a very kind and sincere person. He would speak up if this were bugging him. He would say something to me. I can assure you he's happy you joined us."

Thomas is glad to hear this.

"I guess the four of us—me and Gaucho and Lenny and Margo—we're all trying to figure out what our next move will be. I feel like there are a lot of opportunities. Too many, I think. Some people know exactly what they want. Me, I know better what I don't want."

"A good start, I'd say."

"I suppose," Emelia replies, in a soft and not very convincing voice. "But knowing what you don't want is not the same as knowing what you do want. Gaucho and I talk a lot about this. Gaucho, he's more directed than I am. He has more faith in his future, in his decisions, than I do. Between the two of us, I'm the worrier, I suppose."

Thomas Blake pokes the tip of his toes into the cool sand. He feels the heat from the new day on his neck and shoulders and arms. He runs his fingers through his hair.

"Sometimes, opportunity finds us rather than the other way around," he says. "I believe that opportunity appears from nowhere more often than not. It's sort of a fifty-fifty thing. Opportunity presents itself and you have to seize it, have to act on it. I have a feeling you'll be ready when the time comes."

Emelia leans back and stares at the sky.

Chapter Four

Gaucho builds a fire and makes a pan of migas: scrambled eggs with onions and tomatoes and strips of fried tortillas. A pot of coffee is set to brew. Soon, gracious aromas of coffee spread through the camp, mixing with the salty sea air.

From somewhere off in the distance, across the road in a small village south of Ensenada perhaps, the bells of a church ring in diaphanous harmony—faintly, happily, sadly—calling villagers to morning mass. If for whatever reason you were to go to that village, you would find old women in thin black shawls slowly making their way to the church door. At that village, as in thousands of others like it, this is how it happens in the morning every day of the week.

Gaucho talks effusively of the day of surfing that lies before them. The waves will be tall and ripe and challenging. The kind Gaucho lives for.

The sun is now already smoldering up above them. Thomas Blake leans on his elbow. "Well, today this guy is taking a day off from the surf," he announces. "These old aching bones are like rusty tools that won't move." He rotates his shoulder and grimaces.

By ten o'clock, Gaucho and Emelia and Lenny are on the water. Thomas Blake lies on the sand and looks at the large palm overhead. A song plays on his phone, a song he knows very well. But now it seems to be speaking directly to him. Neil Diamond's *I am...I Said*. For Thomas, the words are truer than ever. Deep inside he does feel lost. Not between two shores but lost just the same. And like the song, he once dreamed of becoming a king...and then became one. His own version, at least. Everything was perfect until that day. That day when.... He stares at the palm fronds that quaver in the breeze. Now it is Billy Joel singing, *Always a Woman to Me*. No song ever captured Kathryn more perfectly.

Thomas changes from his flip-flops into his running shoes and trudges up to the highway. He bends and stretches muscles that are as tight as piano strings. *This might be a slow run*, he tells himself. He glances at the sky as if in search of divine inspiration but sees only transparent clouds left behind from earlier in the morning. Clouds loosely scattered across a solid blue canopy. He leans forward, moans, and takes to the road.

Chapter Five

Saturday night is a buzz of energy as clusters of Mexicans and gringos saunter through the streets of Ensenada. Dinner is at a small café along Avenida Adolfo Lopez Mateo. The room is redolent with the aroma of mole and beans, boiled shrimp and langosta, fried huachinango. Through an open window comes the smell of the chalky streets and the sea air.

After dinner, the four again find themselves in Hussong's. On the way over, they pass the Hotel Casa Del Sol. Thomas Blake remembers spending a night there with Kathryn once when they were going to Cabo San Lucas. The memory of that night is vivid—it could be yesterday. The fun they had had relaxing by the pool, frolicking in bed in the room.

Hussong's is more crowded than ever. In a stroke of luck, they manage to get a table near the wall away from the crowded center and off from the bar where people group heavily. Thomas orders beer. The ever-present mariachis circulate through the cantina. When one band leaves, another promptly enters as they move up and down Avenida Hacienda from bar to bar.

People in the cantina swing to the spirited and soulful notes of the mariachis when they break into an inspired version of *Guantanamera*. Thomas Blake knows the words in Spanish and English.

> I am just a man who is trying
> To do some good before dying.

Horns wail and guitars chirp. The darkly grooved faces of mariachis trill the words, eyes closed, faces to the ceiling. The entire cantina is drenched in the tale of Guantanamera's struggle for life.

A man at the next table lights a cigarette, one of those clove-scented things. A bloom of smoke lingers lazily in the air above the table, blending with the other fragrances that tangle in the room. The creator of the cloud blows three perfect smoke rings that follow each other one upon the next up to the ceiling.

Minutes later, a pair of gringos at the bar get into a tussle. A bigger fellow and a shorter but tougher looking one. The room falls into silence as everyone watches. The mariachis stop playing and sneak to the edge of the room, not wanting to risk damage to their instruments.

From out of nowhere, two very large bouncers wrap the assailants in tight bear hugs and carry them to the door where they are unceremoniously flung onto the street like bags of litter.

Hussong's returns to itself again—happy and noisy.

"Crazy show," Gaucho utters and takes a swig of beer. "All right," he says, "since Brother Thomas is here with us, I have an announcement. Here goes." He pulls in a breath, deep and long, exhales, and says, "I've made a decision."

Guitars again strum as the mariachis break into *Sabor a Mi.*

"I'm quitting my job," Gaucho says and raises an arm as if swearing before a judge. "I'm going into business for myself. It's make or break time for me. That's what I feel. Pretty soon, I hope there will be a shop in Pacific Beach with a sign in front that says: Gaucho's Boards and Gear." Gaucho beams happily as he speaks the words.

Emelia has known full-well of Gaucho's plans. In characteristic thoroughness, Gaucho has thought over every detail, has worked out a plan, and has talked about it with Emelia for months. Gaucho knows everything about the business, having worked in several surf shops for over five years. He knows the products, the types of people who come in, what they want, what they don't want. He knows where to buy stock wholesale, and the right prices for the boards and the wetsuits, the T-shirts, the swimsuits. And he has an extra feature, a special feature.

"I've been making boards in my garage for quite a while now…custom boards. Both of the ones we have today, mine and Emelia's, I made. In the store, I'll have everything. The low-end stuff, the high-end stuff."

Emelia raves about the craftsmanship Gaucho brings to each of his surfboards. The creativity. The style. Already, he has many commissions and a good following. The word is spreading fast.

Though the group swore off margaritas for the night, Gaucho's good news calls for a celebration. A pitcher of ice-cold margaritas and four glasses are set on the table. Thomas fills the glasses. He raises his, looks at Gaucho, and says, "Salud, amigo."

The glasses clank.

The mariachis warble. A young boy carrying a tray with packages of gum and cigarettes weaves through the cantina selling his wares.

Chapter Six

Thomas Blake is up at first light. He walks to the water and sits on the cool sand and stares out over the ocean at a sky cast in a dark pink hue. A color he has seen at other times, early in the morning.

"Red sky at night, sailor's delight. Red sky at morning, sailor take warning," Thomas murmurs.

He doesn't recall what the sky was like the night before, but there is no mistaking it this morning. He thinks about the meaning of that as he watches the waves break and tumble. Big barbarous waves with white ridges that tear to shore.

Looking at the sea, Thomas Blake has an uncomfortable feeling. It could be nothing more than the residue of the margaritas they treated themselves to at Hussong's. The ones they had hoped to avoid. The electrifying atmosphere of the cantina makes it difficult to hold to one's commitment no matter how stubbornly one tries.

Yes, it could be the residue of the margaritas that now taunts Thomas's thoughts, filling them with quiet urgency. But as he stares at the vermilion sky, shoulders hunched, he feels certain it is more than the dross of the margaritas that is toying with his thoughts.

Thomas Blake trusts his instincts. He, like many people, knows that we are occasionally granted tiny insights into the future, visions of what life has in store. That's what he believes, in any case. Premonitions that foretell of occurrences yet to come. Events that loom hours, minutes, maybe only seconds, ahead of us. When these enigmatic feelings emerge, they're never clearly laid out. Rather, they are constructed of shattered pieces and scattered parts that do not make a complete picture. The edges of a jigsaw puzzle that have yet to be filled in. He tries for a moment to locate the origins of these thoughts as he looks out at where the sea melds with the misty red sky. For no obvious reason, he suspects that the answer to his concern lies somewhere out there. But why? What? Is it something destined for him? How is he to know?

He leans on his elbow and begins to hum *I Am…I Said*, the way a familiar song creeps back into your mind a day or two after you recently heard it. He hums the words, then begins to sing them softly. It makes him feel oddly better. *Somehow, we are all lost*, he tells himself in quiet reassurance. *All of us, everyone. Who isn't? Find someone who has been spared this feeling. Are we lost because our dreams never come true? Or are we lost because, in luck, many of our dreams do come true? Which is it? Does it matter?*

He pictures Kathryn's smile. A happy smile, but a worried smile just the same. He remembers it well, this kindly but worried smile she had. A smile that came to her rather suddenly and spontaneously. That beguiling smile da Vinci put on his famous portrait that hangs in the Louvre. Is it a happy smile or a sad smile? Or is it neither of those…or both?

Breakfast that morning is slow and ceremoniously silent. The bells from the distant church peal and fade, peal and fade. Thomas Blake recalls the John Donne quote Hemingway used in the fore pages of *For Whom the Bell Tolls*: 'And therefore never send to know for whom the bell *tolls*; It tolls for *thee*'.

The telltale effects of the night at Hussong's are felt by all. Coffee is taken in slow deliberate sips until the pot is empty and a second is started.

In time, Gaucho says, "Our last day here in Ensenada. The waves are big. We should make the best of them before heading back."

It is almost noon when the boards are put to the water. This time it is only Gaucho and Emelia and Thomas. Lenny will don his wetsuit and bodysurf.

For an hour, the three surfers ride waves in near perfect harmony with the sea. The red sky of early morning is gone, pushed off by an endless ceiling of bright blue. Despite the large waves, Thomas feels more confident than ever. His earlier concerns, whatever their origins, no longer bedog him.

Gaucho adopts a wave and rides it to shore. Emelia is next. Thomas dangles on his board out where the sea is beginning to spiral up before it curls into pipes. To his left,

Lenny appears and disappears, his head bobbing on the undulating water like a floating pelican. Thomas gives him a thumbs up and looks over his shoulder in search of a wave.

All at once, in barely a second, Lenny is being swept out to sea. He screams hysterically as he swims to make his way to shore. He is caught in the deadly grip of a riptide. Thomas turns his board and paddles frantically toward Lenny. If he can get there, he can save him. He is gradually moving closer. The shore seems more distant than ever. Hopelessly far off.

Lenny is torn with panic.

Thomas yells. "Stay calm!" he shouts. Thomas knows there is no hope of swimming to shore when caught in a riptide. The best swimmer in the world couldn't do that. Getting out of it will take a clear head and determination.

A dozen feet from Lenny. Almost to him, almost to him…almost there. He calls to Lenny, telling him to slow up, to save his energy.

"Don't fight the tide," Thomas yells. As he nears, Lenny reaches and grabs the surfboard and pulls it toward him. In a moment of fear, he tries to climb onto it. The board flips, sending Thomas into the water with Lenny. The board shoots away from them into the strong current. Eight feet, ten feet, twelve feet—gone. Lost. Lenny grasps Thomas's arm with a hand tight as the claw of a raptor. The weight of Lenny's erratic motion ties up Thomas's ability to swim. He takes in a mouthful of salty water but manages to keep from swallowing it.

Thomas feels the tension, the sense of fear, that has

overcome Lenny.

"Listen, Lenny!" Thomas screams. *"Listen to me! Listen!* You're in a riptide. You're trying to swim to shore. Don't. You can't get out of it doing that."

This frightens Lenny even more. He flails in the water. "Lenny, listen to me!" Thomas shouts over and over. "Do what I tell you and we'll get out of this."

Thomas knows the way to survive a riptide is to ride with the current. It will move out to sea and then turn and swing back in again. Out, to the side, and in—flowing in the shape of a horseshoe. To panic, to attempt to swim to shore, is certain death. The only hope, the only means of winning, of surviving the tide, is to ride with it and let it bring you to shore. But it's not natural to do this as you're moving farther and farther out to sea.

Lenny grasps tightly onto Thomas's arm. Thomas sees the look of horror in Lenny's face. The eyes of a man staring at death. Lenny is no longer swimming—his arms are frantically thrashing at the sea. He takes in a mouthful of water, swallows some, spits some out.

Thomas pulls Lenny to the side. He senses that the riptide is beginning to move laterally. Yet the shore is horrifyingly far off, almost out of sight. Lenny is losing strength. Thomas knows that if Lenny goes down, they will certainly both go down. But maybe, if Lenny wears out, Thomas can take him by the chest and let the riptide itself bring both of them to shore. It is possible. It will be difficult though. Thomas is a good swimmer, but not a great one. He has no training as a lifeguard. He feels his own strength slipping away. How long can he hold out against the power of the sea? He tries not to think about it.

Looking to shore, Thomas is convinced they are moving parallel with the beach. This is good, yet they still face the dubious possibility of making it in.

Again, Lenny slips into a state of panic. His arms swing and slap wildly on the water in an attempt to fight the tide. Thomas yells, trying to calm him. He needs for Lenny to gain control or there will be little Thomas can do for either of them. Thomas's mind is pressed onto the moment. He can think of nothing else. Glancing to shore, he is certain they are on the edge of the riptide and possibly turning inward. He tells Lenny this as he props him up; Lenny's head is now low on the sea. They will make it, Thomas tells him.

Lenny is limper than ever. Thomas orders him to keep going. Lenny swims, exhausted, in a crude dogpaddle. Slowly, feebly, but it seems to help. Thomas looks at the shore. Yes, now he is sure they are on their way in.

In front of them waist deep in water are Gaucho and Emelia. They know about riptides and they know how hopeless it is to try to swim out to help Lenny and Thomas. They would never make it so much as fifteen yards against the fierce tide that is now gushing in. Emelia's hand covers her mouth.

At last, Thomas assures Lenny they are heading for shore. A few more minutes, just a few more minutes. A few more. Turning to Thomas, Lenny's face draws a fragile smile.

When they are near the shore, Gaucho and Emelia rush out and grab Lenny and pull him to land. He falls on the sand, eyes shut from exhaustion, breathing heavily and deeply.

Part III

Chapter One

Upon returning to Del Mar, Thomas Blake is tormented by endless thoughts of being trapped in the riptide with Lenny, even to the point of having two gruesome dreams. There they are, Lenny and Thomas, far out on the water. Three times they are sucked into the turbulent sea. All about are fish of various sizes and shapes—big ones, small ones, fish with mouths turned up, mouths turned down. Above them is the thin glassine layer of the top of the water, fading farther away. Thomas tries to save Lenny, eyes as motionless as the eyes of the fish around them. Eyes moored to the look of death. Thomas awakes as Lenny is sinking to the ocean floor.

Each evening, Thomas vows to return to the café in the morning, and each morning he knows he cannot go in his present state of mind. Finally, desperate to free himself from the prison of his house, he heads out to Maxine's for dinner. Seeing Carmine's joyful face will raise his spirit, he figures.

He angles his way across the five short blocks until he arrives at the restaurant. The sprite Japanese lanterns that hang on the veranda make him feel better. He smiles for the first time since setting foot in Del Mar.

"Good evening, Mr. Blake. Are we here for dinner tonight?" Carmine rhetorically asks as he enters. She turns and with a menu under her arm starts into the restaurant. "I have the perfect table for you. And how lucky you are, it's over by a big window that looks out onto the sea. Just as you like." She hands Thomas the menu.

"Hmm," Thomas demurs, stopping and looking about. "Carmine…I have a special request tonight."

"Well, of course, Mr. Blake, what is it?"

"This one time, maybe a table over here." He points arbitrarily to the center of the room. "Maybe for a change it will be nice to sit away from the window."

"As you like," Carmine replies with a happy wink. "*Bon appetite!*"

"*Merci.*"

"And shall I have a single malt sent over?"

"Yes, that will be terrific. Yes, please."

When the drink arrives, Thomas sits for a moment carefully cupping the glass as is his habit. He breathes in the fragrance of the malt and takes a sip. Looking around the restaurant, he is surprised at how empty it is for a Thursday night. Normally at this hour, nearly all the tables would be filled. The room would buzz with conversation. But tonight, he is grateful for the soothing quietness around him.

He takes another sip of scotch and feels the glamour of the alcohol as it buoyantly caresses his mood. He thinks about his meal and decides to go for something different. He knows the menu by heart. The flounder, local and fresh, is excellent. So too, the sole meuniere. Or perhaps tonight it will be sea scallops, delicate and lightly sautéed.

The low lighting in the restaurant is comforting. Two lovers at a table nearby talk softly, locked onto each other's words. Thomas glances at the wall of windows where the deck lights glow onto the frothy surf.

Before he realizes it, the two fingers of scotch in the tumbler are gone. He signals to the waiter for a refill. Sipping the scotch, he thinks about Evan Noir. In a strange but delectable way, he knows exactly where the next book will take Evan, if Thomas can make it happen. This is odd because Thomas never writes from an outline, rarely more than the slightest idea. The words come to the page as the novel progresses. Yet, in the next version, the as yet unwritten episode, Thomas knows precisely what will happen despite having shed only a few timorous paragraphs onto his computer screen. Words that each time are promptly sent into the wastebasket of the ethernet. Is this feeling, this sudden confidence he now senses, merely the spirits of the scotch toying with his psyche? Probably, but he enjoys it just the same.

In the last novel, Evan Noir made it to the end by the very barest of luck and came out with a bullet lodged in his chest so close to his aorta the surgeons decided to let it stay for fear of damaging 'some very important real estate nearby'. Evan was on the road to recovery and was ready to fight yet another day. Days in the life of a gumshoe are tough, and Evan Noir is as tough as any that found his way onto the written page. Every bit the equivalent of the classic hard-drinking tough guys that came from the pens of Raymond Chandler and Dashiell Hammett and Mickey Spillane. Thomas realizes—as he has many times in recent years—that Evan Noir's future, his precarious existence, is suspended in bitter uncertainty.

The ambiance in the restaurant is soothing. After dinner, he sits at the bar and sips Pierre Ferrand to finish off his meal. He talks to Jorge and Carmine. He is glad he came to Maxine's.

Chapter Two

Thomas Blake sleeps late the next morning. It is ten o'clock by the time he arrives at the café. Gaucho and Emelia and the other surfers are already off to work. Thomas orders coffee and unfolds the newspaper. Mike, the owner, comes by. He runs a cloth over the table next to Thomas and stuffs a tip into his pocket. Looking at Thomas, he says, "Surfing today?"

"No, not today."

"Gaucho says you're one of the best."

"What a nasty rumor," Thomas replies, coddling a smile.

"They were in here as usual...Gaucho and Emelia and the gang. Didn't see Lenny though."

"How's business been?" Thomas asks.

"The café? Going well. We just celebrated our first anniversary."

"It's a good café. The best in Del Mar, I always say."

"I finally found my calling," Mike says. "I used to work for a biotech over in Sorrento Valley. It's a snap to get people to move here for a job, what with the great weather and all. That's why I came. Moved in from Jersey to get away from the cold and the snow. The job wasn't all that bad, not really, but I was just a cog in the wheel. No chance to go very far. So, I went all out and bought this place and here I am. Not exactly getting rich. But it doesn't matter, I'm doing what I love."

Thomas Blake has a second cup of coffee. The morning is moving toward noon. A group of six come in and study the chalkboard wall menu. They have the look of snowbirds who fled some icebox up north for the warmth of Southern California. If they are in for the season, they're likely holed-up in a place like El Cajon east of San Diego, where temperatures hover between seventy and ninety year-round. Where you can toast in the sun at any time of the year. They purvey the room, hold a small powwow, and take a table.

At that moment, Lenny comes strolling into the café. It's unusual to see him so late in the morning. He looks at Thomas and sits down. Mike brings Lenny his regular double espresso, into which Lenny drops a cube of sugar and gives it a swirl.

Thomas and Lenny talk briefly about the weather, a rather inane topic in a place where the temperature repeats itself again and again, day after day, with no change. Camelot, known to the natives.

After a few moments, Lenny says, "Maybe now isn't exactly the best time to bring this up, but, well…I need to thank you.…I mean about Mexico and the riptide and all."

He clears his throat, hesitates, and thinly adds, "If you hadn't been there, I'd have…well, you know. I'd have—"

"You'd have made it. Somehow I think you would have."

Lenny shakes his head—eyes, moist and sad. In the bleakest voice, he says, "If you hadn't been there…."

"But I was. That's all that matters."

Lenny takes a sip of espresso. He tells Thomas of a chilling dream he's had almost every night since returning from Mexico. It sounds terribly like the ones Thomas has had. The wild thrashing in the water. Sinking to the bottom of the sea. Breathing in large gulps of water, but miraculously not drowning. Filled with the terror of dying, but not dying. One of those pathetic recreations of a true-life event that are at times more horrid than what actually happened.

"This was the week from hell," Lenny stammers. "First, getting caught out in the rip, and then yesterday…then yesterday I got canned from my job."

Thomas gasps.

Lenny gives a dismissive gesture with his hand as if to discard the bad news. He stirs the espresso and takes another sip. "Dumb-ass company is downsizing. That's what they *claim*. Let fifteen percent go…just like that. No warning, no nothing. Just a notice saying that's it, Bub, you're out. Simple as that. Out!" He flashes a thumb mockingly over his shoulder, like being told to take a hike.

"Jesus Christ, Lenny, sorry to hear it," Thomas says. "What about Margo?"

"She's there…she stays. I guess one of us is good for something." Lenny says, shaking his head. "You know how it is at these companies? They always go after the weakest of the lot. Me, I'm Mr. Go-Along-to-Get-Along. In the business world, the survival-of-the-fittest business world, I mean, this is a huge problem for people like me." Lenny's face takes on a submerged look of guilt as he speaks.

Thomas Blake recalls Emelia using those very words about Lenny as they sat on the water's edge in Mexico early in the morning. Mr. Go-Along-to-Get-Along.

Whether we like it or not, we hide the inner workings of our psyche from very few. Those around us see the real person behind this fragile mask we put on. Our surface façade is paper thin, transparent as cellophane, obvious to all. It's often only ourselves we fool. And barely that.

Lenny talks in long slow spurts into which are daubed quiet interludes as he stares blindly around the cafe. "I've been like this my whole life…sort of an empty shell I guess you could say." His brow furrows as if mindfully unhappy with his own comment. "Ah, screw it…what's it matter now?" He looks Thomas in the eye and quite seriously says, "You know, Thomas, you know everything. So, tell me—"

Thomas laughs. "Well, I *sure as hell* don't feel like I have answers to much of anything," he utters, with the most heartfelt sincerity.

"But you do," Lenny prompts. "Tell me, do you ever wonder about life's events? Why they happen the way they do? I thought about this a lot since I returned from Mexico.

Thought about it a heck of a lot."

"Sure...I think about those things, too. All my life I have," Thomas says.

"So, I wonder...see, what I'm getting at is, is there some plan to life, or is it that everything just happens...happens sort of, you know, spontaneously?" Lenny says. "I've never been a religious person, so I don't buy into that Hand of God crap, to put it rather bluntly. Yet, I often wonder, is there really, possibly, some grand plan to life? For example, let's say a squirrel falls out of a tree and breaks its neck and dies. Does anyone believe that God suddenly decided to knock the squirrel out of the tree? Get what I mean?" Lenny rubs his forehead and looks away, as if deep in thought. "It all sounds pretty damn preposterous to me," he says, turning back to Thomas. "Well, anyway, about what happened in Mexico, I didn't tell Margo. She would have freaked. Flat-out freaked! I don't want her to know...ever! But it's sort of funny, actually. Sometimes, Margo tells me she's afraid of the ocean. She talks about how vast and powerful it is even when you're just a few feet out. She told me never to mention this to Gaucho or Emelia. They know all about the water, having been on it since they were little. Now I know exactly what Margo's talking about. Anyway, I guess what I'm getting at is this...is everything we do nothing more than a random toss of the coin? I was saved because you were out on the water waiting for a wave. Had you not been there...well...you get it. What if you had gone for a run that morning instead? Worse yet, what if you hadn't come to Mexico with us? Or what if I hadn't decided to bodysurf that morning and went out there with my surfboard like usual? So many variables. Anyway, the stuff in Mexico, the riptide and all, and now this crap with my job, well, it changed me pretty quick. Margo's been working overtime. Get a load of that. They dump my ass and then work her like a slave. Pretty slick, huh."

"Pretty slick."

"I could have died out in the ocean, but as you said, I didn't. And, yes, those bastards that I worked for could have kept me on, but they didn't do that either. I was doing everything they wanted. Everything and more. My father used to tell me, 'Bust your ass and you'll get ahead.' You know, that old bust-your-ass work ethic crud," Lenny says, trying to make light of it. "Well, I did. I damn well did.... I busted my ass and got fired. Know why? Because some bastard sitting at a desk with a calculator decided the company needs to cut back. But the company is doing fine. The stock has been soaring nonstop for a long time."

"Now what?"

Lenny shrugs. "Do you want to hear something crazy? If anything, all this crap has made me more determined than ever. And I don't mean about scrounging up another job sitting in front of some goddamn computer in some goddamn sterile office. I told Margo yesterday that I made up my mind. I'm going to start writing."

Thomas is floored.

"Well, I have some money stashed away and...see...I'm thinking, weird as it might sound, I'm thinking of moving down to Mexico to give the writing thing a try. At this point, what have I got to lose? What?"

Thomas remembers his early days of writing when he was just starting out. Sitting in his garage with his typewriter set on a folding table he bought at an office surplus store in Solana Beach. The thrill of setting each word on the page. Blindly believing that he was writing a great detective novel. The euphoria of seeing Evan Noir come to life day by day. The naiveté of believing that it would be a huge best seller. Hardly anything compared to the excitement of that.

"Sure, I could stay here and write, I suppose, but I think it will be better if I get away. Sort of shut myself off from all the distractions I'd have in Del Mar. I heard you can rent a place in Mexico, in Ensenada, for next to nothing, and my Spanish is pretty good. So that'll help. I don't know. A part of me is afraid of failing. Afraid of falling flat on my ass and having to come back and be a computer jock for all of eternity." Lenny moans grimly. "Before I lost my job, I had been planning for a long time to start a book. You know, work it into my daily routine. But now that everything fell out from under me, I feel like putting all my energy into the book." He rubs his forehead again and glances away.

Thomas wishes he could share with Lenny his own long and enduring experience writing, the great pleasure it brought him. But he can't. The snare he set for himself long ago as the faceless author Philip Keenly prevents it.

"Who knows, maybe events in our life *do* happen for a reason," Thomas says, immediately wishing he could recover the words the second they are spoken.

"Anyway, something inside me says I should give it a try. One thing for sure, I'm not about to climb on a goddamn surfboard and paddle out onto the water after what happened. But corny as it sounds, I like to think of this as my chance to be like the writers who settled into Paris after the First World War. They went there to write. You might think they'd want to get as far away from France as they could, given all that happened in the war...but they stayed. Christ, they wrote some of their best stuff there. What do you think? Does this make sense or am I just being a dumb-assed romantic?"

As Thomas sees it, it matters only that Lenny puts the time into his writing, wherever he is.

"For two days I thought about this, thought about it long and hard. And I decided just as you said right here, no, I did not die out in the ocean. Though I damn well could have. But I didn't. And I could have been one of those who were spared from getting fired. And then just keep slogging along at a job I hate more each day. But I made up my mind I'm not going to let all that bad crap ruin my life."

Lenny gives the espresso a swirl and finishes it. He looks up momentarily. His eyes sink back toward Thomas. "You know, I like Southern California, but often I wonder if I'm really meant to be here...if it's the right place for me is what I mean. You've been here a long time. Right?"

Thomas shrugs and nods.

"So, I guess this is home for you then. I've been here

for a little over five years now and...I don't know if it will ever be home for me. When you grow up in the frigid north, it turns you into a funny sort of beast."

Thomas ardently agrees.

"You lived somewhere cold?"

"Oh, yeah, many years ago...Boston. Do you detect the accent?"

"A little."

"You can't get rid of it, I suppose."

"Like speaking Minnesotan, as we call it. So maybe this going to Mexico thing will be good for me in a lot of ways. A chance to live somewhere else, I mean." He considers that thought for a second and says, "Well, Margo is here to stay. That much I know for sure. You'll never find her back up north. Or out east. Or anywhere else, for that matter. Not Margo. She may not be too thrilled with her job, but she loves the life out here. We're sort of different that way. About Southern California, I mean. Well, as for the book, I have only a vague idea for the story."

"Evan Noir mysteries?"

Lenny laughs wildly. "Hell no, I can do better than that! No, it's about some kid who moves to Southern California from Minnesota," he says, grinning and gloating. It sounds good for the moment. "Like I said, I wrote a few stories. But a novel...that's a whole different critter, I think. What if I run out of words before it's done?"

"Well, here's what I think. I've always considered a novel to be nothing but a string of short stories put together end to end. That's how I feel when I read a book."

"Truth is, three times I tried to start a novel and three times I failed," Lenny says.

How many times had Thomas tried to get his first novel going? A lot more than three. Not to mention all the attempts that died ingloriously after no more than a few paragraphs. But, then, how many successful writers haven't had similar experiences at one time or another? Hardly any. Thomas Blake knows that the way to beat this is to do what he did with his first Evan Noir book. Write the entire story beginning to end with little or no revisions. Write and fix later. That became Thomas Blake's approach for every one of his books, and it always worked. No outlines. Very little planning. Just the barest idea of a story. Let it move forward on its own—with a few fitful and tormenting moments along the way, of course.

Lenny gets up to leave. For the first time all morning, his face glows.

⋏

Thomas walks down Tenth Street until he arrives at his bungalow. He continues on and stands above the ocean and looks at the blue sheath that spreads far into the distance, a couple walking hand in hand, a pair of pelicans that skim inches above the water.

He thinks about Lenny's decision to start writing and about how bravely he dealt with the dire event on the ocean in Ensenada. The situation with his job that greeted him when he returned.

For a second, Thomas wonders whether young people are more resilient than older people. Nah, he doesn't believe that, not a bit. Or is there possibly some truth to it? This thing about taking risks—big risks, little risks. It's part of the reason governments send young people to war. They, the youth, all believe they'll return. Older folks know better. Is there, then, a modicum of resiliency that is bequeathed on each of us early in life, and when it's gone, when it's used up, there is no more? If so, what happens when it *is* gone? Can we purchase a new order? Have it magically bestowed on us and apply it to our future?

For almost three years, everything in Thomas's life has been painfully grafted to the relentless memory of Kathryn. Lenny could have let the down-turned episodes of the past week tarnish his future, but he didn't. Lenny—Mr. Go-Along-to-Get-Along—got up and marched forward. He started over again. Can Thomas do the same?

Chapter Three

Lenny wastes no time relocating to Mexico. He gathers the minimal essentials of life, throws them into the back of his truck, and locks down the canopy top over the truck bed. He gives Margo a kiss and a huge hug and sets out. He will make trips back on weekends, or she will come to visit him periodically as things progress.

Lenny bursts with enthusiasm as he drives along the coastal highway of Baja. He barely remembers passing Rosarito, the usual waystation for a brief stop. His thoughts are nervously but joyfully fixed onto the life that awaits him.

By noon he is in Ensenada. He grabs a quick bite at a street-corner taco stand and immediately begins his search for a place to stay. Most of what he saw on the internet before he left was far too pricey. The costly stuff for the well-to-do vacationers. This won't do for him. He needs something essential but efficient. He parks his truck on a safe street, not quite sure where to begin.

The midday sun is direct and stubbornly hot. After an hour up and down one street after another, he goes into a small pharmacia where he purchases a cold bottle of orange

Topo Sabores. Sipping the drink, he reads through a cache of advertisements pinned to a board on the wall: jobs, trucks and cars, auto repair shops of all kinds, tires galore, new and used. And, lo, three notes about houses for lease, each with fuzzy but sufficient pictures of the interior and exterior. Two of the houses look good. One seems perfect. *Will it be available*, he wonders. He snaps a picture of the address and phone number and goes outside. Sitting on the sidewalk, he leans against the building and taps the address into Google Maps. "Is this for real!" he utters, in little more than a whisper. A good location in central Ensenada, yet just out of the thick of things. He calls the owner. They can meet in twenty minutes.

The house is a small but quaint adobe place. Nice kitchen, not modern but not ancient. Bedroom, living room, and a bright and cheery front room with two windows that open onto the sidewalk and street. Behind the house is a teeny yard surrounded by fruit trees and one lone palm that rises thinly to a burst of fronds. The house is simply but adequately furnished and, remarkably, it has internet access, something Lenny worried might not be available.

They discuss the terms of the rental. For the amazingly low price of sixty-five dollars a month, it's Lenny's. He wastes no time signing the forms. Two hours later, his truck is emptied and he's moved in. He sends off a text to Margo telling her of his great luck in locating the house. She is ecstatic.

In the afternoon, he makes a trip down the street to the

mercado where he buys food and bottled water and other essentials he will need to get started on his writing journey.

He fills the refrigerator—pint-sized by American standards—with his purchases, and then spends the rest of the afternoon organizing the house, dubbing it Mi Casa. He goes from room to room, out to the front of the house, into the backyard garden, snapping pictures that he will send to Margo.

The next two days are spent arranging the confines of his new domicile. From a discount furniture store, he buys a cheap sofa and a simple desk, not fancy but ideal for the front room that will become his writing nook. Throughout it all, he does not open his laptop so much as once, and he won't until he is ready to give his writing the diligence it deserves. Lenny is a creature of habit. His world spins in the same direction all the time. He wants his mind to be clear and ready for his first time at the keyboard.

The internet service is connected. Far from warp speed, but faster than he imagined for Mexico. Every day, he sends multiple messages to Margo, updating his progress on the house, and every evening they talk on the phone. Each time Margo grouses about being the one who is trapped at the computer job, and about how lucky Lenny is to be doing what he truly loves. "Oh," she moans. "What envy! What envy!" They talk about Lenny's would-be book, which has yet to have so much as a theme, so much as a cast of characters, so much as a single paragraph of written words.

That evening, Lenny makes a pot of chili that will provide dinner for several days. He sits in the kitchen eating chili with a stack of fresh tortillas bought at the tortilleria around the corner from Mi Casa. My God, they're good, these tortillas! The packaged ones he gets at the supermarkets in San Diego are never as flavorful.

Evening wears on. The warm breeze of the afternoon that fluttered in the windows and coursed through the house has chilled. Lenny locks the windows. He needs a beer, but he recalls his conversation with Thomas Blake in the café on the day he told him about his impending move to Mexico.

"One thing I can tell you," Lenny said back then, "I'm staying clear of Hussong's. You can bet on that. That place may be fun…but it's lots of trouble if it becomes a habit. And the margaritas…aye, yai, yai!"

"Yes," Thomas replied. "Trouble for sure. The plan is to write like a great writer, not drink like a great writer."

Lenny crossed his heart and made a vow.

But now, a beer or two at one of the local bars can't hurt. A mere two blocks away is a place he passed several times. La Barracuda. He knows nothing about it. He throws on a light jacket and heads down the street and walks into the bar.

Darkly lit, the room holds the odor of a well-frequented watering hole—the smell of beer and liquor that are seared into the walls and floor, the muted scents of people that cannot be erased from the air itself.

As his eyes adjust to the dim light, everything begins to

slowly takes shape. To his right is a simple wooden bar with plain wooden stools. Behind it, a bartender polishes mugs and glasses with a towel that he periodically snaps onto his shoulder. Bottles of liquor line the wall behind the bar. A half-dozen tables cluster close in the middle of the room. A large silver-blue stuffed barracuda hangs on the opposite wall. Black impassionate eyes and an oversized mouth. Pinpoint studded teeth. Evolution's fearless hunter. Surrounding this, dozens of flags are pegged to the wall. Mexican, American, German, French, Italian, British, Russian, Japanese, and numerous entries that are unidentifiable but to the occupants of their respective countries.

Ah, ha, Lenny thinks. He has landed in one of the expat bars Ensenada is known for. He walks over and sits at the bar. The bartender sails a paper coaster in front of Lenny. "Buenos tardes, amigo."

"Buenos tardes," Lenny replies. He looks at the row of beers on display in front of the tier of liquor bottles. "Un Modelo, por favor," Lenny says. "Con limón."

The bartender pops the cap off the bottle and pours half of the golden-brown beer into a glass. Lenny drops the slice of lime into it.

The bar is sparsely occupied. Groups of three or four sit at the tables. The language is English, Spanish, other languages. The talk is refrained and quiet. An old jukebox from days gone by and a weathered pinball machine decorated with images of scantily dressed women on an upright glass screen huddle near the wall.

Lenny takes a swig of beer and wipes his lips on his sleeve. For the moment, he is the only one at the bar, but soon two guys and a woman come in and take up residence to his left. American possibly—not Mexican, European or Canadian, he considers. They talk as quietly as the others in the room. Seemingly deep into a conversation of sorts. A simple discussion at best.

Someone from one of the tables goes to the jukebox and drops a coin into the slot. Presently, in a volume toned down to the necessity of the bar, Joe Cocker's gritty voice asks, *"What would you do if I sang out of tune?"*

The bartender prepares drinks for the trio next to Lenny. It's clear they're regulars—insolubly connected by habit to the establishment. The drinks are set out. The bartender flips the towel onto his shoulder and sings with Joe Cocker.

Lenny's spirits are high. Sitting at the bar, he decides that tomorrow will be the day he starts writing. But what will it be? He still has little in the way of a story. Yet, in some osmotic way, the embryonic beginnings are starting to form. Write about something you know, he tells himself. Isn't that what they say? The eternal advice given to all beginning writers. But what can that something be? His life with Margo and Gaucho and Emelia…and even Brother Thomas? Their simple if at times tattered lives in Southern California? In Del Mar? Who will want to read that? There has to be a crisis. A resolution to the crisis. What will it be? Write the book and don't worry about the audience, he concludes.

As he sits deep in thought, slightly hunched over his beer, one of the trio next to him says, "Welcome to The Barracuda. The Cuda it is to us." He shakes Lenny's hand. "New here, huh?"

"First time."

"Thought so. We know the usual bunch that comes in here. So, passing through Ensenada, are you?"

"Moved in this week."

The man raises an eyebrow. He introduces himself and his two companions. "Let me guess...surfer," he says, looking Lenny over. "That's what brings most young folks to Ensenada. Where are you in from?"

"Del Mar."

"Know it well. Just up the road a bit."

"Yes, up the road a bit," Lenny says.

"Two hours."

"About that."

The man nods and tends to his drink. "They say the surfing's good here. So I'm told, anyway. Wouldn't actually know, never having done it. Most of the surfer bars are down by the water. Over by Playa San Miguel there are loads of them...the surfer bars. This here, The Cuda, is a pat bar. Expats, mostly. Totally different creature from the surfer bars," he says, with an airy laugh.

"I'm not really down here to surf," Lenny explains.

"Didn't think so, being originally from Minnesota and all."

"How the hell did you know that?" Lenny says, squinting and giving the man a sidelong glance.

"Did I get it right? I'm pretty good at deciphering American intonations. When you've moved around as much as I have you get to know them all." The man beams at his success. He waves to the bartender and has another Modelo sent to Lenny.

Lenny listens at some length as the man prattles on. Lenny tries to place his accent but doesn't have the repertoire of experiences for that. New England perhaps. Could be New Hampshire or Maine, Vermont possibly. Though he could just as easily be from somewhere outside the US— New Zealand or Australia. If so, much of the original down-under twang is gone.

The man explains that he's worked all along the west coast, even doing a stint on a fishing boat in Alaska. He claims to have no set roots. And doesn't want any. For now, he's settled into Ensenada. His vernacular is as strange as some of the stories he relates, tales that are now and then salted with words like "cad" and "chap" in reference to someone he met along the way.

"Life has changed...too much swirling uncertainty up in the states," he sharply declares, "depending upon which cad is running the show in Washington, of course." He goes into a rather long iteration of why he likes Mexico despite the ills that forever afflict the country—the pockets of poverty, the illiteracy, the petty crime. "The people are good, and that's all that matters to me."

Now and then the woman interjects a thought. From what little Lenny can patch together, she is married to the man. The other, the third person, is a compadre, it seems. Tall and lanky, he stands and leans on the bar and listens to the conversation, saying little except to randomly nod in agreement.

Lenny is having trouble figuring the trio out. They seem unusually interested in talking to him, though they just met him. Is this what expats are like? Even so, Lenny enjoys the encounter. The evening wears on. More dated music flows from the jukebox. Always a classic piece of one type or other. *Ripple*, *Imagine*, *Blue Jean Blues*. That stuff.

Lenny stays later than planned. Walking home, the evening is cool and pleasant. A hint of sea air. The sky glows in shades of crimson. Sailor's delight.

Making his way down the still streets, Lenny thinks again about his book. A theme is emerging. The short encounter with the pats helped. An idea he can work with. A topic he has been considering for a long time, for years, but didn't know how to shape the story. The American dream. The disillusionment of Americans. Does the American dream exist? Or is it a grand hoax that has infected Americans from the days of the early settlers? A means of surviving, of getting through tough times? That and nothing more?

He feels content and good and tired. From the house, he sends a short text to Margo, then falls into a long and deep sleep.

Chapter Four

Thomas Blake makes an appearance at the café just as Gaucho is leaving for a meeting with a man about a surf shop in Pacific Beach. Emelia remains. She opens a book and looks up and sees Thomas. He comes over and sits down and glances at the book. There it is. An Evan Noir mystery.

"Lenny was right, this crap is pretty good stuff. I want to see how Noir is gonna get his butt out of the mess he's in," Emelia says.

Thomas picks up the book. He remembers writing it, though he can barely recall where it fits into the chain of the Evan Noir novels. Early in the series is all he remembers. Fourth or fifth probably. He reads the plug on the back cover. Evan Noir is in a heap of trouble. This time, it is he who is the suspect of a murder—Noir himself. The perfect set up, the perfect stooge. The sleuth who always seems to be around when something bad is going down. Evan Noir needs to move fast. Find the real killer before he himself is dead. Head down in an empty fifty-five-gallon oil drum behind a skid-row bar. He is in a race against time.

"Well, I suppose you heard that Lenny took off for Mexico," Emelia says.

"I heard, yes. I ran into him here a week ago," Thomas says, setting the book down. "Christ, I've never seen the guy so upbeat. The dude's usually like this," holding his hand out as straight and still as that of a surgeon. "Must be some Minnesota thing. The computer crap got to him a little too much, I guess."

"Guess so."

"I can sure understand that. What could be worse than writing programs for a bank? Good lord, what could be worse than that?" Thomas says. He waves to Mike for coffee. "It's a touchy business these days, so I'm told. Most writers barely scratch out a living. Some, not even that."

"Sure, but you never know. That's what they always say, isn't it? Failure is guaranteed for those who never try. Let's see, some old guy I once knew told me that. You live the dream, right? You get knocked down and get back up. Some guy I met in the café was real fond of that idea. Don't remember his name...Brother something...Brother something...." She sends Thomas a quirky smile.

Thomas grins and nods. "You're right. As the great Wayne Gretzky once said, 'You miss a hundred percent of the shots you don't take'".

Mike brings the coffee. Thomas holds the cup to his lip and breathes in the aroma and takes a sip, rather like his routine with a good scotch or a cognac before tasting it.

Emelia looks at the clock on the wall and shoots to her

feet. "Oh, cripes, got to get moving. I'm taking the morning off to run an errand." She picks up the book and her phone. "*Ciao!*"

Thomas leans back in his chair. Seeing the copy of his book pulls again on the inner feeling he can't shake. He wonders when the feeling will finally leave him. *If* it will finally leave him. What if the answer is never? Do we move past these calamitous times in our life? Or do we just bury them? Cover them up? Paper them over like hanging pretty wallpaper on top of a cracked wall. Only we know the cracks that hide below.

Three young surfers come into the café. Happy. Awash with energy. Hair streaked by the sun or colored to an artificial shade of flaming orange. Spiked hair that stands straight up like on the back of a startled cat. They appear to have just come from the ocean. Thomas knows the surf is high at this hour because he's considering getting out on the water later in the afternoon when the waves have flattened to a mere three feet. Safe for his old bones.

The surfers sidle up to the counter. Despite the early hour, they order beer—Corona. They belt down large gulps and belch and laugh one after another. All of them have that look. That look Thomas has come to know well. The strange and unique countenance of a California native. Gaucho and Emelia have it. Lenny and Margo never will.

Thomas drinks his coffee.

Chapter Five

Emelia drives north on Highway 101, cuts over to Highway 15, and continues up to Escondido. She can make the trip blindfolded, having done it so many times. She parks her car and walks to the rear of the condominium, knowing her mother will be sitting under a large umbrella by the pool. It's a routine as predictable as the tides. Twenty minutes in the sun covered in a layer of SPF 25. Forty-five minutes under the umbrella. Repeat and redo.

"Morning, Tanzy," Emelia says, standing over her mother who is spread out on a deck recliner. Everyone, even Emelia, calls her Tanzy. A moniker dating back to a bit part she once had in a grade B movie.

Tanzy squints and looks at the silhouette next to her. "Well, hello dear," she says dryly. "What brings you here?"

"Just thought I'd stop by. It is okay, isn't it?"

Tanzy laughs a little. "Of course, dear. What a nice surprise. Here, take a chair. Is everything all right?"

"It's fine. I've been known to stop by just to see you, and—"

"Are you still seeing...."

"Gaucho."

"Yes, Gaucho." Tanzy always considered the name peculiar, if not a little silly. "Yes, Gaucho," she says again. "You're still seeing him, then?" It comes across sounding terribly unpleasant. As if Emelia is paying visits to some convict in federal prison. Like those people who feel sympathy for an incarcerated total stranger. Weekly visits. Conversations across a sheet of two-inch plexiglass. Something like that.

"Yes, I'm still seeing Gaucho."

"And everything is fine then?"

"And everything is fine then," Emelia replies, grinding her teeth quietly, having to endure the mockery of Tanzy's ritual. "Yes…everything is fine."

If Tanzy is nothing else, she is gorgeous for her age. Barely forty-five, she is lean with naturally blond hair that requires only a touch-up here and there. Constant skin care has rid her of even the slightest blemish. Oh, but in spite of it all, Tanzy is high maintenance. Very high maintenance. Pure trouble for any man who dares to enter her sacred space. Plenty have tried. Plenty have failed. Even there, sitting around the pool, are a half dozen who rolled snake-eyes at one time or another.

"And so, Gaucho is…fine. And you're fine. Well, how nice, dear."

"And you Tanzy, what about you?"

"Oh, you know Tanzy, she keeps plugging along," she replies in the weird way she has of referring to herself in the third person.

Emelia pages briefly through one of Tanzy's magazines. She sets it on the flagstone deck and looks quickly at the sky and then glances surreptitiously at her watch.

Tanzy persists. "So…why the visit?"

Emelia sighs ever so slightly. She is becoming exasperated. A new tact is needed. "Well, yes, you're right. I do have a small matter, well…a little info maybe—"

Tanzy listens. Careful not to commit to anything unnecessarily, she bears that bivalent look she acquires when Emelia is about to ask for a little money, a small loan.

"Okay, now I know this is a bit of a sensitive matter," Emelia says. "And I'm not here to tick you off. You understand that, I hope."

Tanzy waits, barely breathing. Not so much as a blink of the eye. Head angled down, her eyes focus on Emelia over the top of large sunglasses. Finally, unable to wait any longer, she says, "You need a little money…something like that?"

Emelia emits a faint gasp. Of course, that's what Tanzy would think. It is always a matter of money.

"Look, if you and, uhm, Gau—"

"Gaucho. But before you go there, it's not about money, and it's not about me and Gaucho."

"Well, tell me then, dear."

"Dad. I want to know where he is."

"Your *father*?" Tanzy blurts.

"Yes."

"Oh lord," Tanzy grumbles, making it sound as if this is going to be a very difficult and complicated issue.

"You must know where he is. Am I wrong?" Emelia asks.

Tanzy's face falls dead. She offers up a bitter and indifferent shrug.

Emelia wants to scream. Why is this so difficult? A simple question. Does Tanzy know where her father is, or doesn't she? Emelia always feels as though he is somewhere nearby. She has no rational reason to believe that. One of those gut instincts you have when it comes to information that is important to you. At a minimum, Tanzy must know if he is close or far away.

Tanzy slides her sunglasses onto the top of her head. Her green eyes gleam against the umber-brown of her face. "What is it you want to know?"

"His address."

"No, I mean why do you want to get in touch with him?" Tanzy chafes.

"It wouldn't hurt for you to just give me his address, now would it? Without having to go through this ordeal?"

Tanzy has the look of someone being handed a subpoena. "You know what a creep he is, don't you?" she says, in a voice charged with irritation. "You know—"

Emelia holds her hand out, all but blocking Tanzy from finishing her sentence. "That has nothing to do with this," she insists. "I'm making a simple request of you. That's all."

Tanzy groans and thrusts a lock of hair over her shoulder. She closes her eyes and takes in several slow breaths. After a moment, she looks at Emelia straight in the eye.

Calmer, seemingly transformed, she gets up. Hands on her hips, wearing the skimpiest of bikinis, she shakes her head and says, "He's over in Rancho Santa Fe, just across the glen from here. And as you might expect, I *do not* carry his address around with me, *sweet* as he is!" She looks punishingly down at Emelia. Swiveling sharply around, she storms off to the condominium. "I'll get it," she says, speaking over her shoulder.

She returns and hands the address to Emelia on a sticky note. Arms folded, lips pursed, she glares at Emelia.

In barely half an hour, Emelia is driving along the posh streets of Rancho Santa Fe. Block after block of stunningly charming houses with Mexican tile roofs, varietal palms, a splash of flowers in lawns as well kept as the links on an expensive golf course. Bountiful and peaceful.

She follows Google Map until she arrives at the address. The house is indeed spectacular, uniquely designed to blend perfectly with the environment. Emelia remembers Tanzy once saying, in the most curt and sarcastic voice, "Your father lives well, real well, high on the hog. Always has, always will. Porsche, Mercedes, Lexus. Nothing less. I don't think he can afford it…the house, the cars, the lifestyle, I mean. He's a real high roller."

From the street, there appears to be no activity in the house. He might be at work, being midday, mid-week. Emelia turns off the car and sits with her hands on the steering wheel, rethinking her decision, tempted to dart off in a quick escape. To speed away and return to Del Mar.

The front door opens. Emelia's heart flutters. A Hispanic woman steps out and snaps a rug several times on the front porch. She gives a suspicious look at Emelia's car, turns, lifts a shoulder, and goes inside. The door clicks shut, sounding cold and final.

A tear trickles down Emelia's cheek. She sweeps it away and takes in a soft breath. If she were to go to the door, if her father were to come out, would she recognize him? Would he recognize her? Would he close the door in her face? How could he? But what if he did? What if he did? What if?

She sits almost motionless for twenty minutes. Someone peeks out the window of the house and pulls the curtain shut again. Turning on the car, Emelia grabs the steering wheel and drives in a daze back to Del Mar.

Chapter Six

Gaucho walks the palm-lined streets of Pacific Beach with Simon Carneros, a man he has known for many years. Carneros owns several small stores and shops scattered throughout the San Diego suburb that sits just below La Jolla. PB to the locals. In many ways, this is the real mecca for surfers in San Diego. Streets clean as a sun-bleached seashell. Bungalows of white or pale pink. Tidy shops.

Every house, whether a block from the shore or ten blocks in, is accessible to the ocean. Tailor-made for a ride on the water before work, a ride after work, hours and hours all weekend long. A culture of surfing dominates life in the small close-knit community.

Simon Carneros has a list of places to show Gaucho, each ideally suited to Gaucho's needs. "You know the old adage about real estate," Carneros says. "Location, location, location. Well…location I have."

Gaucho is flushed with excitement and uncertainty. No shortage of surf shops do they pass. Some big and flashy. Some small and simple. Places that sell expensive boards, boards for beginners and boards for pros, custom-made

boards. How can Gaucho possibly compete? Can PB tolerate yet one more surf shop? Can it? Don't most of these
places really survive by peddling T-shirts and swimsuits?
Isn't that what Gaucho will end up being? A peddler of T-
shirts to the conventioneers who make the requisite trip
from downtown to PB? The snowbirds who need a souvenir
for that neighbor who picked up their mail and watched their
house while they were away?

Still, Gaucho will be living the dream. Running his own
shop, his own store—*Gaucho's Boards and Gear*. That's all that
matters. He thinks for a second about Lenny in Mexico. He
is living his dream too. Embarking down that empty road,
leaving behind a distant past. And yet, every dream we have,
no matter how glamorous or how plain, brings with it an
uncertain future.

"I'm kind of worried, there are loads of surf shops already," Gaucho pensively says, as they pass two within a single block.

"And lots of surfers," Simon Carneros reminds Gaucho.

"But it's still a risk."

"You make custom boards, right? That'll help a lot. You
have something special. Then, once people are in your place,
they'll buy something. Maybe not a board, but something.
That's always how it is. A shirt. Swimsuit. *Something.* You'll
do fine."

Simon Carneros leads Gaucho through three stores, all

empty and ready to be leased. Any of them would fit Gaucho's needs. One is close to the water, just a block from Mission Boulevard. The second is three blocks in on Grand Avenue. The third is on Bayard Street, also close to the water.

Gaucho will go back and discuss what he's seen with Emelia. Like everything they do, they will make the decision together.

Chapter Seven

Lenny sits at the desk in the front room. Fragrances of jasmine and honeysuckle drift in the open window. This, now and then, laced with smells of tortillas and sweet breads from the corner bakery. Bells peal for morning mass from somewhere off in the distance. Staring at the blank screen of his laptop, hands on the keys, he begins typing:

> Billy Thaler had one goal in life—to be rich and famous. Already, he had the look of someone who, if perhaps not rich, could easily be mistaken for someone famous. Eyes, deep and brown, were accentuated by waves of thick dark hair. A straight nose and an angular jaw held a smile especially well.

Little by little, while running errands in Ensenada and from the nightly visits to The Cuda for a beer, the structure of the book emerges. Something akin to John Updike's Harry 'Rabbit' Angstrom. Something about an ordinary man's belief in his own success. And no one is more ordinary than Minnesota-born Lenny, complete with his perfectly stocked toolbox for dealing with the ups and downs that life doles out.

Leaning back in his chair, he reads what he pecked out. "Christ," he moans. How can he possibly write an entire book? His fingers tap the keys until several more paragraphs fill the screen. He rereads those quickly and continues, staying at it for most of the morning. When he is done, he has just over twelve-hundred words. Not a monumental accomplishment, but a beginning nonetheless.

In the afternoon, he turns off his laptop and traces the streets down to Playa San Miguel. As he watches the surfers dart across the white collar of foamy surf, he has a terrible urge to be out there with them. Certainly, his near-death experience from the earlier trip to Ensenada, and the vow he made not to get back on the water, are a warning against tackling the waves at Playa San Miguel. And yet he is doing fine in Ensenada. For the moment, all the little pieces of his life seem to be fitting together. How can anything go wrong now?

On the way to the beach, he passes a small surf shop. He knows that all shops have used boards that can be picked up for ten cents on the dollar. It so happened that, at the last minute before leaving Del Mar, almost mechanically, he tossed his wetsuit in the back of his truck, making it all too clear that he had no intention of remaining true to his promise of avoiding the surf.

He eats lunch at a small café near the beach and afterwards returns to the surf shop. Sure enough, a few used boards, all in good shape and no worse for the wear, rest against the back wall. And priced to fit into his pocketbook. He selects one and pulls out a roll of pesos.

⅄

For three days, Lenny keeps to his writing. Each morning before starting, he sits in the backyard and reviews what he wrote the previous day. He always makes sure to end at a place where he can promptly start again in the next morning. It's a trick he heard about, and it seems to be working.

Billy Thaler is coming to life—edgy and smart and cool and handsome. Determined. An American. Twenty-two years old and barreling headlong down that narrow path that leads to the future. If anyone is going to make it, it will be Billy Thaler. The more Lenny writes, the more he likes this Billy Thaler person. He is like Lenny himself. Roots set shallow in Midwest soil. Roots that are easily transplanted. That's what Lenny is after in Billy Thaler. The wanderlust that is seared into the soul, the marrow, the DNA of Americans.

In barely a week, Lenny has added ten thousand words. Whether Billy Thaler's story will make it to the end of the novel, Lenny has no idea. Will it be like a wave that starts out brazen and tall and gutsy and then after a massive splash returns to the sea and becomes a rolling whimpering swell, soon to vanish? A mere thimble of its former self? Will the story of Billy Thaler be like that? Each morning Lenny wonders, worries.

Every day at noon, he gets up and stretches his stiff legs and frees himself from his work. He meanders through Ensenada, navigating his way past the old stucco houses and the brightly painted new ones. Aromas of tortillas and tacos and enchiladas surround him. He slips into a small restaurant for a light lunch.

One day as the sun hangs heavily over Ensenada, he takes his surfboard and sets out for Playa San Miguel. When he arrives, he sits on the board for a long while and watches the waves as they plume up and attack the shore. *Maybe this isn't such a good idea after all*, he thinks. His confidence at the keyboard fuels confidence with the surfboard. Is it a smart move or a stupid move? He isn't sure. He doesn't have Billy Thaler's daring, his aplomb—the utter confidence that Lenny has conferred on him. Billy Thaler brims with all the natural attributes that Lenny himself thinly owns.

Half an hour passes. Forty minutes. Lenny gets up. Surfboard under his arm, he trudges to the sea and paddles out where, steadily straddling the board, he waits for a wave—the right one, a good one.

Chapter Eight

The Cuda is near empty when Lenny enters at just past eight in the evening. He sits at the bar and orders a Modelo and dips a tortilla chip into a bowl of pico de gallo. He pokes the wedge of lime into the beer bottle and takes a slug.

Someone is playing the pinball machine. Bells chime as the steel ball ricochets around the table, bouncing from knocker to knocker. Music falls from the jukebox. Fleetwood Mac, *Don't Stop Thinking About Tomorrow*. Lenny thinks about tomorrow. He is as happy as he has ever been. All he needs now is a visit from Margo and his simple life will spin free and wonderful. She will be down on Friday, just two days away.

Four people come into the bar and sit at a table. Soon after, two others enter. The room brims with chatter and laughter. By the time Lenny is on his second beer, the trio from his first night at The Cuda stroll in and sit next to him in the same order as before: man, woman, man, to the left of Lenny. The talkative fellow wears a Hawaiian shirt splattered with sunny tropical leaves and long-billed toucans. No sooner have their drinks arrived than the man looks at Lenny and, with a dab of laughter, says, "Well, if it isn't the chap from previously. Good to see you, old buddy. Good to see you."

"And cheers to you as well," Lenny says, with a tilt of his beer, attempting his own version of the man's strange patois.

"Now tell me, how's the surfing going?" But before Lenny can correct him, the man follows with, "Wait. Got it wrong. Sorry, old boy. No surfer here. Am I right? If you were, were a surfer is what I mean, you wouldn't be hanging out at The Cuda. You'd be over at Hussong's…some place akin to that. Or at one of the spots over by the beach…San Miguel."

Lenny opts not to mention his afternoon of surfing.

"I'm trying to figure out what you do," the man jauntily says. "It's sort of a hobby of mine. Like the fellow at the circus who guesses your height and weight. But I don't do that. No Kewpie dolls to give away if I come up short. I like to guess what people are up to. And I'm pretty good at it." He turns and looks at the woman next to him. She nods, rather unconvincingly. Returning to Lenny, he says, "Now don't get me wrong, I'm not a snoopy person." He leans back and crosses his arms as though thinking hard. Lenny doesn't mind. He finds it all very comical.

"My first impression is something with computers. But I'm not going there because it's an easy guess. Everyone works with computers these days, don't they? But just the same, here goes. You were a computer pilot and now you're down here in Ensenada to…let's see…you gave up the computer shtick and you're writing a book."

Lenny nearly chokes on a mouthful of beer. "Christ almighty, now how in the hell did you know that?"

"Got it pegged, did I?" he says, leaning a little toward Lenny. "A gift you could say. I probably *should* be in the circus. Who knows?"

"All right. If we're playing guess the profession," Lenny says, "what's an expat do for a living? Shall I guess?"

"I'll save you the trouble. Not much of anything."

That makes no sense to Lenny. Aren't expats supposed to be so disgusted with what's going on around them that they pack up and leave in protest?

"You see, fundamentally expats are malcontents," the man says in an apologetic drone. "We leave behind what we can't fix or are too lazy to fix. I won't kid you, it's a cop-out. Talk to any of these folks." He points around the bar as if he can account for everyone there. "We won't admit it, but that's how we ended up here. Or over in Vera Cruz, or Madrid, or Costa Rica. See how transparent it is. We think we're protesting the system, the system we claim we can't support. But truth is, no one gives a bloody damn we're here. I know it. I haven't fooled a soul…least of all myself."

This greatly troubles Lenny. His inner sense of duty wants to hear that there is something oddly noble in what they're doing. Something that will make a difference in the world.

A long string of clamorous chimes ring from the pinball

machine, to the point that Lenny turns to see what is happening.

"You can't tilt it," the man next to Lenny explains. "Impossible to. You can lift the bugger up and shake it all you want, but it won't tilt. The tilt gizmo has been turned off, or it's broke. I don't know which. The thing is one big pain in the arse, to my way of thinking. A while back, some chap came in here and played it all night long. Ping, ping, ping, ping, ping…all night long," the man says in obvious disgust. "Ruined the usual peace and quiet of The Cuda."

Lenny orders another Modelo.

"So, tell me, what's this book you're writing about? A little sneak preview perhaps so that when it becomes a bestseller I can tell all the expats I met you right here in The Cuda. I should mention, this isn't just an expat bar. There are a fair number of writers who congregate here as well. See, I cheated a bit when I pretended to take a stab at your profession. I made a good guess based on the phenotype of the bar—the fact that it's both an expat bar and a writer's bar."

Lenny doesn't divulge the theme of the book. He knows if he does he will fall prey to a tsunami of suggestions for the book from a total stranger. But there is one benefit from it. His protagonist, Billy Thaler, is as much an expat as any in The Cuda. And that Lenny likes. Day by day, Billy is shaping up nicely.

Chapter Nine

Thomas Blake sits in the café with Emelia. The others have left. She will need to be on her way soon as well. Three previous mornings she could have told Thomas about her failed attempt to see her father, but she said nothing, and now she feels more remorseful than ever. Thomas, she hopes, will be able to share a word of advice, some support, console her if nothing else. She told Gaucho about her trip to Rancho Santa Fe. He was sympathetic and comforting, yet she is still filled with disturbing emptiness.

"I got his address from Tanzy," Emelia says in a flat voice, explaining to Thomas who Tanzy is. "I drove to Rancho Santa Fe and sat in my car in front of his house. A maid came onto the porch for a while and went back in. I sat there, gutless, unable to go to the door, and then, hopeless, I drove home. It was the worst day of my life," she says, her words crawling with emotion. "Strange, all the while until that very moment, I thought I would have the courage to go right up to the door. To knock on it. And he would come out and would be happy to see me. Overjoyed even. That's how I imagined it. I created a story that's never ever going to happen."

"I think you should go back," Thomas says, gently but assertively.

Emelia stares off to her left. An absent stare. She shakes her head. Her silence is amplified by the emptiness of the café that morning. "I'm better if I just accept it the way it is," she states.

"But you don't want to, do you?"

"No…I don't want to."

"Then don't."

"What can I do?"

"You can try again."

"And then?"

"And then it all might work out."

Emelia considers this. "Do you think so?"

"I don't know. We can only hope. I have no crystal ball. Often I wish I did." The words lead Thomas unexpectedly to his own dilemma. Is it better to accept things as they are and move on? Or are we, humans, forever conscripted to the notion that there is some tangible meaning to this emotion we call hope. The belief that change really does takes place, and with luck it will be for the better.

"I wish I knew, too," Emelia utters. "If I go back and try and fail, I'll be destroyed."

"You'll know you did what you could. That's important"

"And then I can move on. True?"

Thomas agrees.

Emelia sighs. She starts to speak but stops. With great sadness, she says, "Why is life so damn miserable sometimes? I'm not asking for a miracle. We want from life what we can't have. Is that the rule? Sometimes, a lot of times, I think about my friends and think about the families they have. And I get jealous, I won't deny it. Maybe I'm asking for too much from life. Gaucho has a good family that he is close to. And Lenny and Margo also I think, even though their families are off in Minnesota somewhere. Tanzy and I have never been close, and I don't have any brothers or sisters. And now, to make matters worse, there's this thing with my father."

"Maybe your family is right here. Your friends. The people in the café."

Emelia nods reluctantly. "But still…you know what I mean." She looks drearily away again. Thomas waits for her to speak. In a while, she says, "And to make matters worse, I still have that dream about my father. I had it again just the other night. Exactly the same. Always on that swing. Always him singing that song. So gently, so rhythmically." Emelia's eyes grow moist. She gets up. "Well, that's where I am." Permitting a small smile, she says, *"Ciao,* Thomas. Off to the mines for me."

Emelia leaves the café and walks up Camino Del Mar toward the boutique on Fifteenth Street, angry at herself for caving in and driving away from her father's house. She could have gone to the door. Could at least have done that.

Knocked on the door. Waited for someone to open it. Found out if her father lives there. Maybe, if he wasn't there, could have learned when he'd return. But now, after talking to Thomas, she is determined to go back. Thomas is right. She has nothing to lose. The worst of all possibilities is that the visit will put a sad end to the whole bitter episode.

She glances at her watch. Her pace quickens. The day is wonderful. The blue sky is getting richer and brighter by the second. The sea breeze is fresh, tantalizing. Almost gone is the morning fog as it crawls eastward where it will disappear over the mountains in the Anza Borrego desert. Perhaps today she will take the afternoon off and make a trip to Rancho Santa Fe. Perhaps.

The boutique has just opened when Emelia arrives at exactly ten o'clock. The owner is standing in the doorway looking westward to the sea that is fused in a deep shade of blue with the sky. It is Friday and the boutique will be busy. Despite the simplicity of Emelia's job, she likes the work.

Emelia gets along well with the owner. Maybe someday Emelia will have her own boutique, but for now she is content to work at the store. She realizes how much goes into being a proprietor of even a small store. This already has become evident to Gaucho. The worries and concerns that go with it. The difficulties in getting and keeping help you can trust. And yet, Emelia knows that Gaucho is happy. He has never been happier. This brings joy to Emelia.

"Hola," Emelia says.

"Hola," the owner replies. "A bright and beautiful day."

She wedges a doorstop under the door. Warm and fragrant air swims into the store. "I'm thinking that soon, maybe next week, we need an inventory."

"Of course," Emelia says. "Whenever you want."

The store has done well. It draws in locals as well as tourists. Lots of expensive clothing. Expensive and stylish. Fridays are always busy. Saturdays, busier. Sundays, the busiest of all. Emelia's hours at the boutique are spread out comfortably across the week.

All morning Emelia's thoughts return to her conversation with Thomas at the café. His gentle encouragement to try again. Will this afternoon be a good time for that? Tomorrow? Is Saturday better? Emelia considers this as she folds and stacks shirts and tank tops on a table and organizes skirts and dresses on a rack.

Behind her someone is humming a barely audible tune. She stops and listens. How uncanny, how strange. That song. The one from the swing set. The one from her dream. Turning, Emelia sees a man standing a few feet away. Tall, tanned. She stares at him for a second, unsure of what to do. Unsure of what to say. She waits.

"Emelia?" the man says.

Emelia is unable to speak. Eyes wide. Mouth open. *Is this? Can it be?* For a second, she wonders if it is a trick, a cruel gimmick someone has come up with. But who would do that? Is it really her father? She hasn't seen him since she was fourteen. She takes a timid step forward. The man holds his arms open, waiting for her. Now she is certain. She walks up and wraps her arms around him, unable to hold back the tears.

It is nearly noon. She tells the owner she will be back in an hour.

They go to a restaurant just a short way from Fifteenth Street. It's busy, but they get a table without waiting long. As they sit sipping iced tea, waiting for their sandwiches, Emelia's face glows. Her father explains that he has been trying to find her. He says Tanzy told him that she, Emelia, had moved away, somewhere out east, and that she's in and out of trouble. It is nonsense, of course. A complete lie. Why Tanzy would say such a thing is unclear. Just to spite Emelia's father, no doubt. Then, the maid told him someone was sitting in a car in front of the house. She managed to get the license plate number as the car drove off. Her father traced it to Emelia.

Part IV

Chapter One

Months pass. Springtime leaps onto center stage in Del Mar, bringing with it wonderful days and pampered evenings and balmy nights. Thomas Blake keeps to his plan of preparing for the Del Mar to La Jolla half marathon. One recent evening when he met up with Patrick Simmons at Maxine's, he made a foolish vow to run the race, and now he is committed and feels he can't back out. Patrick Simmons will hold him to his words.

"I'll watch you vanish in front of me as you charge up the hill at Torrey Pines," Thomas Blake plaintively said to Patrick Simmons.

"And I'll hear you on my heels about to pass me up," Patrick replied.

It brought a good laugh.

Thomas Blake recalls those words as he changes into his running shoes and shorts and T-shirt and takes to the streets of Del Mar and down Highway 101 past Torrey Pines Beach. It feels good to be out. The morning is early; the air is soft and dry.

Little has been heard from Lenny since he moved to

Mexico except for the occasional update brought back by Margo from her visits to Ensenada.

Returning from his run, Thomas pours a tall glass of cold water and slumps into a chair on the front porch. He tilts back and closes his eyes and breathes in the sweet air filled with the aroma of honeysuckle. When he opens his eyes, coming up the walk is none other than Lenny, briefcase in hand.

"Buenos dias, amigo," Lenny says, sitting in a chair next to Thomas.

"My God, if it isn't the long-lost Lenny," Thomas crows.

Lenny's face is tanned. His hair, bleached by the torrid Mexican sun.

Thomas Blake can hardly wait to hear how the writing has been going. He desperately wants to ask, but rather, he will wait for Lenny to tell him. After all, what if it was a disastrous mistake, a bad decision, a god-awful blunder?

But there is no need to wait because Lenny jumps in immediately, saying, "Thomas, I want to tell you, I think it went pretty well."

"The writing?"

"Yes, the writing."

"The book...the novel, you're saying?"

"Yeah, the book...uh-huh."

"And...?"

"I worked hard every day, just as I promised. It wasn't easy. Some days were torture. Then other days, the words seemed to come freely. I have no idea what I've accomplished, though. That's the problem. I guess, if nothing else, I learned a lot about this writing stuff. We can never be the judge of our own work. We can never determine whether it's good or whether it's total crap."

Thomas Blake knows this too well...Lord almighty, does he ever!

"And how far did you get?" Thomas asks. "On the book?"

"I'm almost finished."

"You must have put in a lot of time to get so far so quick."

"Peace and quiet, no interruptions, no visits to Hussong's. I did make it to a bar around the corner now and then, however. It's a good bar...just a beer or two for me, no tequila." He tells Thomas about The Cuda, and about the expats, and how he became friends with several of them. "And, of course, Margo came down most weekends and that helped a lot. I didn't want to start making trips back to Del Mar. I was afraid I'd get sucked into the lifestyle here and end up spending less time in Ensenada."

"So then, about the book...?" Thomas asks. "Or would that be too much for me to—"

"I'll do better than that. I have a very special request." Lenny says. He picks up the briefcase. "I need someone to read this thing. An opinion," Lenny says, unaware of Thomas's long writing life. "Would you be willing to? I'm not interested in any editing. Nothing like that, mind you.

Just a neutral pair of eyes. I need an honest opinion. And I mean *honest*, truly honest. You read a lot. Am I right in that?"

Thomas nods.

"Okay, let's just say you bought this book at the bookstore and started reading it. And—"

"No problem. Done."

Lenny reaches into his briefcase. With a nervous smile, he pulls out the manuscript and hands it to Thomas. "Remember now, honest opinion. All right? If it's crap, for Christ sake, *tell me*."

"Honest opinion. Yes."

Lenny and Thomas sit on the porch for hours. Thomas brings out a pitcher of iced tea. Lenny talks about Ensenada and more about The Cuda. The expats. How he really doesn't understand what it is they're up to, but that he enjoys them just the same. He tells Thomas about the handful of writers who come to The Cuda. Most of them as uncertain in their quest as Lenny is. But all filled with boundless determination.

Thomas discusses the Del Mar to La Jolla that's not far off. He tells Lenny about Gaucho's surf shop in Pacific Beach.

"It's going well, I hear," Lenny says. "That's my boy, Gaucho. He'll do okay. I have faith in the kid. He knows the surfing business better than anyone."

Chapter Two

Thomas Blake's curiosity can wait no longer. Within half an hour after Lenny leaves, Thomas is fifty pages into the manuscript. The character of Billy Thaler is taking shape. Tough, street-smart, gutsy and cocky, and yet strangely humble. There is a kindness to Billy that is likable. An amazing blend of sophisticated complexity. Thomas Blake cannot stop reading. Each chapter, each page, sucks him farther into the book—a riptide that pulls him this way and that.

Thomas has no idea where Lenny acquired his writing skills. Yet every year, new writers, unheard of writers, splash onto the literary scene with great books. Every notable writer hit the bookstores with a big first success. Norman Mailer, *The Naked and the Dead*. Saul Bellow, *Dangling Man*. Many others. And now, here, Lenny Stark's Billy Thaler is searching for something as elusive and erratic and fleeting as the wind that blows in off the ocean.

By four in the afternoon, Thomas has read the entire manuscript. Only a few short pages are needed for Lenny to finish it. How it will end is anyone's guess, but it doesn't matter. Lenny accomplished more than Thomas could have imagined.

Thomas leaves his house and goes to the cliffs that peer down onto the ocean at the end of Eighth Street. The sun is genuflecting off to the west. The ever-present surfers are there, darting across the top of the sea. Dashing and curling back and forth.

But this is not why Thomas Blake came to the sea—not to watch the water or the surfers or the fading orange sun. He is there to think, and think hard, about Lenny's book. What Lenny will need is a publisher. Thomas, of course, has an editor in the form of Sam Morini. Should Thomas mention the book to Sam? What harm can it do? Or perhaps he should first discuss that with Lenny.

Thomas Blake pulls his cell phone from his pocket, rolls through the contacts, and taps the personal phone number for Sam Morini—the number that many times Sam has hoped will have Thomas at the other end with the news Sam so desperately wants to hear.

The phone barely rings once. "Thomas, old pal, what's up buddy?"

"Sam, I have a big favor to ask. Did I catch you at a bad time?"

"Never a bad time for Thomas Blake," Sam barks.

"There's a young man out here with a damn good book," Thomas says.

This is not what Sam is hoping for.

"His name is Lenny Stark and he's written a book that

will knock your socks off. And believe me I'm not exaggerating, not a bit. This is it. The great American novel. Maybe the greatest ever."

"Those are pretty hefty words, Thomas."

"I know, but he's done it."

"And he's an unknown?" Sam quickly interjects. "Do you know what it's like trying to peddle that to the publisher here? Not to mention to the world? I'd rather have a good Evan Noir hot off your laptop."

"You're still a hell of a bad shrink, Sam."

"Bad, but damn persistent."

"Back to the book, now," Thomas says. "You need to take a look at this. I'm serious. What have you got to lose...what?"

"Does he have an agent," Sam asks, trying to find some room to maneuver.

"I doubt it. He just finished the book. Finished it pretty fast, I must say. For the moment, I'm his agent, I suppose."

"New business endeavor for you?"

"So, if I get him to email you a copy of the book, will you look it over? That's all I'm asking."

Thomas Blake knows Sam will agree. He thanks Sam and tells him he won't regret it. He slips his phone into his pocket and watches the theater of nature and mankind unfold below him. His thoughts fall back to his own dilemma. Once again that very morning, before he went to the café, he walked into the small room where his books are lined up on the shelf. It's like walking into a museum. He hates it because it is not a happy feeling. He turned and left. Too painful to be there.

Sitting on the cliffs, he thinks about Lenny. He thinks about Gaucho. He thinks about Emelia. Each with a personal challenge that they faced directly. Why can't Thomas do the same? Perhaps he hasn't really tried. Yes, perhaps he hasn't. It is possible. Perhaps he doesn't want to. Doesn't want to bring Evan Noir back to life again. Is it because if he does it will bring him back to a time in his life when everything was as close to perfect as possible? When he and Kathryn were together, happily? When his life seemed perfect? But life is never perfect. We only get brief moments that trick our psyche into believing life will always be this good. Was Sam Morini right when he told Thomas to go on a long trip? Something that might pull him from the past and set him firmly in the present? Like it or not, we live only in the present, soiled as it often is.

Thomas climbs down the path that leads to the beach. He sits for a while on a sandstone mound and watches the surging ocean and the sky as it melts into a thousand shades of peach and lilac and lavender. He rests his forehead on his fingertips and closes his eyes. Strangely, as if coming in a whispered voice, he hears:

We cannot change what was.
We cannot prevent what will be.
But we can still live today.

Who is speaking to him? Thomas is not a religious person. Throughout his life, he rarely confronted thoughts of the afterlife. We live. We die. We're gone. That is his belief. And when we are gone, we might live through the lives of others we left behind. That's the only afterlife Thomas believes in. Whether we live in the lives, the memories, of thousands of people, as happens with someone famous after they're gone. Or in the memory of just a few, those who were close to us. It is the only version of the afterlife Thomas believes in. The one he treats as sacredly as any notion that comes from the pulpit.

Thomas looks out over the ocean. He gets up and walks to the water's edge. Barefoot, he lets the cusp of the sea caress his toes before it retreats again into itself. Then, like a cat touching an unfamiliar form, it once more sneaks forward and strokes his toes. Over and over. He walks into the water to his knees. Even standing in the shallowest perimeter of the sea he can feel its wily mood tug at him.

Thomas Blake knows now what he is going to do. He is ready to act.

Chapter Three

Thomas is up as the first beam of sunlight spills across the sky. He has no plans to go to the café. He makes a pot of coffee and sits at his desk and turns on his computer. Sipping coffee, he glances over at the small snapshot of himself and Kathryn that hangs on the wall. It is the middle of winter and they are on vacation in Colorado, ankle deep in snow. The Rocky Mountains loom in the distance.

Thomas clicks on the Word program and sets it to a blank page. He types seven simple words as though they're sent to the page on their own:

Evan Noir was in trouble, big trouble.

Another sentence goes down and then another. Soon, his fingers flick across the keys as fast as ever in the past. He doesn't stop to revisit what he has written for fear of losing the moment; the words carry themselves. The stream of writing sails quickly forward. Even in the best of times he rarely experienced such fortune with words. Time flies by with impetuous urgency, with interruptions only for coffee refills.

Before he knows it, he is on page eighteen of the double-spaced manuscript. Along the bottom of the computer screen is the entry: 4126 words.

Thomas Blake leans back. He grins and shakes his head as if pulling himself out of a dream. He is afraid to go to the beginning and reread what he has written. Afraid that it will be pure gibberish. A pile of incoherent thoughts and nothing else. But he does. By the time he is on page three, he begins to laugh. It has the usual choppy parts that first drafts always have, but Kathryn would have loved it. Evan Noir is indeed in trouble. How in the hell will he make it out of this?

He pulls an Evan Noir book from the shelf above his desk. One from the middle of the series. Opening it randomly to a page, he reads it, places it back on the shelf, and does the same with another. From this one, he reads the first two pages. He repeats this with two more books. He picks up the printed pages he wrote that morning, expecting to find his efforts to be nothing but a sullied version of what he accomplished back in the heyday of his writing career when everything was going well. When Evan Noir was entrenched in a dire search for a serial killer, walking a thin line of danger. But as he reads his latest budding episode of Evan's encounter with truth, honesty, and the American way, all he can do is laugh at what a humblingly good job he has done that morning. He knows now that he can finish the book, and that it might be—just might be—the best Evan Noir ever.

Thomas looks up at the picture of himself and Kathryn,

smiling, standing in the snow. This time, he will keep his promise to her. When the book is published it will have the name Thomas Blake in big letters on the cover. A picture of him on the back. A short splash describing his many years of writing Evan Noir mysteries under the name of Philip Keenly. It will be dedicated to Kathryn. Acknowledgments to Gaucho and Emelia and Lenny and Margo, and the mornings at the café, all of which brought Thomas back to life. He is happy. But most of all he knows that if Kathryn were there with him, she would be ecstatic. And that is all he needs to know.

At midday, Thomas goes for a run in Del Mar. A long run. Success at the keyboard is like a rapturous gush of adrenaline that courses through his veins.